The Old Wooden Rocker

The Old Wooden Rocker

The Illusion of Family
Book One

A Novel by

JEANNETTE SEIBLY

MOUNTAIN
OWL
PRESS

The Old Wooden Rocker
The Illusion of Family
Book One

A Novel by Jeannette Seibly

ISBN: 978-1-7353504-3-1 (Print)
978-1-7353504-4-8 (eBook)

Library of Congress Control Number: 2021920833

Book Design: Nick Zelinger, NZ Graphics
Editor: Lizabeth Netzel, Fresh Ink
Book Coaches: Suzanne Sell
Dr. Judith Briles, The Briles Group

Published by: MOUNTAIN OWL PRESS

FICTION / Family Life / Women's Fiction
First Edition

Printed in the United States of America

Note: The town names of Berlin, Ohio; Harrison, Illinois; Red Fox River; and West Northern Railroad are fictitious.

The Illusion of Family Books

The Old Wooden Rocker, Book One
A Mother's Greatest Regret, Book Two

Other Books by Jeannette Seibly

It's Time to Brag! Business Edition
The Secret to Selling Yourself Anytime,
Anywhere: Start Bragging!
Hire Amazing Employees
Be a Fabulous Podcast Guest (and get invited back!)

In memory of my mother and father,
and their ancestors.
May they all rest in peace, love, and forgiveness,
releasing their regrets.

Prologue

We're all aware that we inherit our DNA from parents, their parents, and back through time.

Often overlooked is our inheritance of beliefs, habits, and actions. Family traditions die hard, if they ever do. They create an illusion of family togetherness. They determine how we act towards one another to avoid risking removal from the family. Those who choose a different path become black sheep. This occurs even though the perspectives of the outsiders can actually expand the definition of family unity.

Family membership is often dictated by those with the most money or who are the most controlling. Others must follow their lead to stay part of the group. Many do follow blindly along, believing their actions or decisions were fated, while merely reliving tradition.

When inherited family pathology is ignored, it continues to haunt us in the present.

George and Catherina Gunther arrived in the small community of Harrison, Illinois, in 1886 and became an important family there. They came with hope in their hearts and a vision in their minds of how to create a promising family legacy, one that transcended their forefathers' traditions and mistakes.

They believed in a new destiny of hope, hard work, and success for all, a life built on family unity to last for generations to come.

But those dreams unraveled on one beautiful sunny June day. Money and greed became more important than family unity. The fated family tradition prevailed.

Thread by thread, the tapestry of George and Catherina's dream unraveled.

As in so many families, each member lacked the courage to create a different destiny for generations to come.

Gunther & Schoenly Genealogy

Herman Gunther m. Mathilde Snyder, each immigrated to America from Germany
m. March 1, 1856 in New York state
Sabrina (b. 1857; married)
Leroy (b. 1858; married)
George (b. 1862) m. Catherina Schoenly
Joshua (b. 1863) m. Molly
Sadie (b. 1864; married)

Henry Schoenly and **Joseph Schoenly,** brothers, immigrated together to America from Germany

Henry Schoenly (Papa Henry) m. Gertrude Linck
m. February 20, 1859 in Berlin, Ohio
Children: Catherina, two sons, and two younger daughters

George Gunther (1862 to June 11, 1939) m. **Catherina Schoenly**
(June 30, 1866 to November 11, 1950)
m. July 4, 1884 in Berlin, Ohio
Children:
Magdalena Catherina (Maggie) (April 8, 1885 to May 11, 1950)
m. Nathan Landes (d. 1950)
m. July 4, 1903 and div. 1916
Child: Nathaniel (b. 1909) m. Linda Farmington (b. 1912)
m. 1935
Children: Sybella and two sons
Henry Joseph (8-16-1886 to 8-18-1886)
Jacob (b. 1888) m. Merry Schneider (b. 1889)
m. 1906
Peter (b.1891; married)
Benjamin (b.1894) m. Constance Whitley (d. 1937)
m. 1919
Rachel (b. 1898) m. Albert Shoemaker (1883 to 1935)
m. 1926
Matthew (b.1899) m. Grace Ziegler (b.1898)
m. November 18, 1917
Children: Susan Helen (b. November 11, 1918)
Emma Grace (b. April 20, 1921)
Paulina Rose (b. October 30, 1925)
Patricia (Patti) Elise (b. June 1, 1930)
Charlie (b. 1900) m. Melinda Brelsford (b. 1900)
m. 1918
Children: Jessica and three sons

PART 1

We honor our traditional family beliefs in the decisions we make today, many times to the detriment of one another.

Catherina – May 1884

Catherina stood in the doorway of the small cabin and looked out onto the muddy courtyard. She inhaled the fresh air rinsed clean by the rain. Papa Henry had been caught in the backfield with the oxen. She smiled as she watched him and the oxen shake their heads as they walked sedately up the lane to the barn, refreshed from the warm shower on a hot day.

Her attention was drawn to the birds' twittering as they skimmed and dipped across the puddles. Everyone was enjoying nature's bath.

Even her garden looked greener already. Papa Henry often teased her about her "little field," as he called it, but was proud of what she accomplished. She loved watching the seeds burst through the soil and nurturing them to pop out their leaves and offerings. Her prayer was to cultivate an abundance of peas, carrots, beans, cabbage, lettuce, radishes, tomatoes, cucumbers, squash, and watermelon. Starting in a few weeks she would be able to start harvesting these treasures and take them into town to sell along with her embroidery. It was her way of contributing and fueled her dream about this becoming her farm someday. But now she didn't know if that could happen.

Tomorrow, she planned to plant the squash and watermelon from her seed collection, if Papa Henry didn't need her working in the big field.

She nervously grabbed the broom and swept the already swept floor. It would take time for Papa Henry to unhitch the oxen and finish his other chores, which included feeding and watering the milk cow, horse, two pigs, and two work oxen. Grinning, she thought about the mangy mousers and stray dog that would show up too. The chickens and two tame rabbits had been fed before the rain started.

Papa Henry nodded and smiled as she waited on the porch of their cabin and watched him walk up from the barn. She smiled in return and inhaled the warm air. She nodded to the east when he got closer, and they watched a rainbow disappear with the setting of the evening sun.

The smell of wild rabbit stew and sourdough bread awaited them. Papa Henry used the lye soap to wash his hands and forearms at the old white metal basin before sitting down across from her. It was now just the two of them. Her two younger brothers had fled several months ago when the winter gray turned into spring sunshine.

After they had both eaten a few bites and slathered butter churned earlier in the day on the warm bread, he said, "Minister Herzer came to see me when I was in the field earlier this afternoon." He'd been attending the local German Methodist church since his brother and he each married a local girl and started farming here.

Catherina nodded and sighed.

After Papa Henry had eaten another bite of stew and bread, he continued pointing his fork at her. "He mentioned that George Gunther asked about you. He's looking to get married."

After he swallowed, he continued, "He wanted to know what I thought about it. He added that he'd encourage it since there are only a couple of good single farmers left in the area. But they're too old for you."

Catherina offered a small smile. Then she said, "George was here this afternoon too. He mentioned wanting to get married and wanted to know if I'd be interested." She shrugged. "I don't know."

Papa Henry finished eating and stood to pour himself a cup of coffee from the blue tin coffee pot next to the fireplace.

"You could do worse," he said.

"Ja …"

"The Gunther family isn't rich. But they aren't poor either." Papa Henry sat, thinking it through. "But I'd be concerned about what'll happen when Papa Gunther passes. There are three sons. As you know, the oldest gets everything. In this case, the whole farm, all 90 acres."

He paused and sipped his coffee. He wanted to add a shot of whiskey but thought better of it since this was an important conversation.

Then he continued, "I don't know what George has planned since he's the second oldest son. Leroy, the oldest, isn't cut out to be a farmer. The younger brother too … he is interested in farming. Minister Herzer mentioned George has the dream of being a big farmer. There's not enough land to divide in three and make George happy."

He paused and nodded to the baked apple pie sitting nearby. She smiled and cut him a piece.

"Your ma and I have done our best to prepare you to be a farm wife, but your independence and outspokenness might get in the way of any man from town wanting to marry you. And there aren't many single ones around here either. Even though your ma was a town girl, she didn't think you'd do well to try and fit into town life."

Papa Henry finished his pie. He sat and watched her eat her pie before adding, "You're a hard worker and can't sit idly around. God knows there is plenty to do around here. But I'm not your future. You need a family of your own. People to take care of you when you are old and enjoying your old wooden rocker." He smiled at his attempt to joke.

Catherina sat still for a while, her face emotionless, then stood up and cleaned up the table and dishes before returning to her seat at the long wooden trestle table. She patted her hair to make sure it hadn't escaped its bun at the back of her head.

"George mentioned his dream too," she said. "He also told me Minister Herzer said I was well-schooled in reading, writing, and arithmetic. It's why he thought I'd make a good farm wife." Catherina had tears in her eyes. "But is that what you want for me? What will happen to you? You can't live here alone." She felt her duty was to her Papa Henry since her mama and sisters had died, and her brothers fled.

Papa Henry laughed. His deep voice resonated throughout the small cabin. "My dear child, I've lived alone longer than you've been alive. Your uncle Joseph is widowed and his farm is next to mine. We're two old men who will be fine. The truth is, I don't have a dowry for you. George and his family are good church people and will accept you without one. I'm willing to give George these 20 acres of land, but your uncle Joseph and I have already offered our farms to your brothers. They don't seem to want them. But that could change."

He paused before adding, "If your brothers don't return, I'd want to be sure George got the farm, not Leroy, after all the work your uncle and I have done. It's hard to say what

Leroy would do with it since he has no interest in farming and is only interested in prospering for himself."

He paused and watched the firelight dance across the hearth.

He added in a kind tone, "I've not seen other men knocking at the door. Soon you'll be 18 and will be thought of as too old to marry. You don't want to be known as an old spinster, do ya?"

Catherina sat and watched the flames. The evening had turned cool and she gathered her mama's old shawl around her shoulders. She didn't know how to put into words what she wanted to say. Her biggest fear was her Papa Henry would think less of her and she wanted to please him.

"You're right," she said with a grim smile. "I wouldn't be living far away if I married George. In fact, we share a property line with the Gunthers on the other side." Catherina tried to think of good things that could come from the union while her heart broke.

She would still be close enough to tend her little field and make sure her papa was well cared for. But her dream of being "a farmer" in her own right would vanish. She was afraid to share it with Papa Henry out of fear he would laugh and call it nonsense. He'd tell her it wasn't right for a woman to have the same dreams as a man.

Being married wasn't her dream. It just wasn't what she thought about, even when her mama and younger sisters were alive and talked about preparing for marriage. But the truth was she didn't dream about being a large farmer owner either.

Her biggest fear was George would decide to leave the area in the future. What would happen to Papa Henry and Uncle Joseph without her to help them and ensure everything was done right?

And this farm suited her just fine. It was manageable. But today young women were expected to get married, bear children, and support their husband's dreams. Would that be enough for her? *It would have to be.*

With her feelings all mixed up, she stood and walked over the wooden floor to kiss Papa Henry's cheek good night.

"Do you want me to turn down the lamp?"

He shook his head and scratched his whiskers. He'd moved to the old rocker that had been his wife's and was thinking about what needed to be done tomorrow.

After Catherina pulled the cloth barrier around her bed in the corner of the cabin, she changed into the cotton nightgown she'd embroidered. She climbed onto the feather mattress held up by a rope and four wooden posts that kept it off the wooden floor.

She lay down without moving until she heard her papa snoring, then turned and put her face into her pillow to allow the quiet sobs and hot forbidden tears to flow.

"Is this all there is to life?" she whispered to herself. She wished her mama was still alive so she could ask her what was best.

George – March 1, 1886

The dawn peeked over the horizon as a tear dropped from George's bowed head. He held the ragged leather gloves that had belonged to his pa. His forefinger traced one of the small holes that had worn through the top of one soiled brown glove. It brought back memories of the years of fencing, birthing livestock, and other farm labor they had shared.

He missed the old man. It had been a surprise to find the gloves under his bench seat on the wagon. His ma must have placed them there yesterday before she left—a goodbye gift she knew meant a lot to him. It was most likely the last time they would see one another.

As the sun rose higher, the pink and yellow clouds moved through the sky, announcing a bright new day. There was a chill in the air from last night's dusting of snow. It glistened on the tree branches, barn roof, and wooden fence rails, so fresh and new, like the journey he was embarking on with his wife and daughter.

George inhaled the scent of spring, an earthy mixture of damp soil and grass stems awakening from their winter hibernation.

Spring had come sooner than normal to northwestern Ohio. The grass and early wildflowers were peeking their green heads out of the soil. The snows had begun melting in mid-February, leaving the lanes rutted and roads muddy, but not impossible to travel on.

George Gunther believed the roads were dry enough to allow his two wagons to get to the main road that ran into

Defiance, along the Maumee River. He hoped the hickory wood wheels would withstand the long journey and not get stuck in mud or standing water. They needed to meet up with the wagon train in town, the day after tomorrow to join others on their journey to north-central Illinois. The plan was to arrive in late March and begin spring planting in mid-April.

The thought of fulfilling his dream and owning his own farm brought a sad, but excited smile to his face. It meant leaving behind his community and birth family. But the promise of fulfilling his own legacy outweighed any fears.

He had become a tenant on his parents' farm after his marriage. His eldest brother, Leroy, had inherited everything as the oldest son when Pa died the previous year. Leroy had sold everything ... the Gunther family home, barns, land, livestock, and the tenant cabin. George found out by receiving a notice that he would need to vacate. But he'd been struggling with a decision of whether to stay or go and took the notice as a sign.

As he thought back to last October, it had been after the final harvest when he traveled to the heart of northern Illinois to a small town called Harrison. He had heard at the General Store in Berlin about a farmer wanting to head west to seek his fortune in gold. George had wired the man and received a telegram back the next day.

A week later he arrived at the 200-acre farm. Peoria was a city that would be about a day's ride south and Chicago was about a day's ride north in good weather. The farm was close to the small town, appeared to be growing, and had grain collection points at the railways and river. He anticipated this would make it easy to get his grain and corn to market during harvest season. The farmer told him Peoria was north of the state's capital, Springfield, where Abraham Lincoln lived before becoming the 16th president of the United States.

George was glad the barn and granary were in good condition. Like many farmers, he was more concerned about the outbuildings than about the condition of the house. He knew Catherina would fuss—not so much about the condition of the place, but as a distraction from missing Papa Henry and Uncle Joseph. They had refused to join the couple in their move westward. George had made sure the house was in livable condition before agreeing to make the purchase. He hoped this would make the move easier for her to accept.

He also planned to fix it up after the planting and the harvesting seasons during the upcoming years.

Part of the land was already cleared. In future years, he planned to expand the acreage through his sweat and that of his yet-to-be-born sons. As a gifted carpenter, he would build Catherina the furniture she desired to replace the items that would need to be left behind.

While George had heard that steam-engine trains were a faster way to travel, he believed it was cheaper to move everything himself. When he talked with the wagon master in Defiance before heading to Harrison, he learned there would be other families traveling via covered wagons to settle in Illinois. And there would be single men with only their horses and backpacks wanting to strike it rich farther west in the Rocky Mountains. All would be part of the wagon train he and his family would join the day after tomorrow.

George sat on the wagon seat with the reins dangling from his hands. With his six-foot height, he had to stretch out his long legs and grimaced when his shoulder and back muscles hurt. While he was normally strong, he was sedentary during the winter months, and all the recent activity reminded him of it. He took off his hat to run his hands through the dark brown hair that his wife had trimmed a couple of days ago.

As he got comfortable, he gazed at the beautiful dawn as if in prayer.

No red skies today. A good sign. He smiled to himself. God was good. Time to move on out. He watched in wonderment as the sun rose higher, bit by bit.

His final decision was difficult. It meant leaving his birth family and familiar German community in Berlin. But once his decision was final, Catherina and he had focused on preparing for the move with hope in their hearts and a vision in their minds of a better future.

It was a necessary move to fulfill his dream. His own legacy. He wanted to prosper and have his own big farm, not live like so many local farmers here in Berlin, only subsisting year to year. If he'd been of generous heart, he'd have thanked his older brother, Leroy, for creating the circumstance that forced him to leave. But he kept his thoughts to himself, as was his way.

Turning with care so as not to signal the oxen to move and trigger a sore muscle, he looked back to see if Catherina was ready.

"Time to get a move on," he said softly.

He shivered and felt the bite of the cold damp air on his face as a sudden breeze came up. It reminded him that winter hadn't made a final decision of whether it was over or not.

He shook off his feelings of restlessness waiting for his wife. She reemerged after one last look to make sure they hadn't left anything in the cabin, and gasped as she gazed up at the beautiful sky being painted by the rising sun with pink, yellows, and blues.

Impatient to get going, he sighed and gruffly shouted, "Let's go!" She gave a quick nod of her head.

They had to get into Defiance by nightfall and set up camp for the evening. He planned to buy staples from the local general store tomorrow and let the animals have a day of rest before embarking on the long journey. There was no time to waste.

George

As George continued to wait on his wife, he remembered saying goodbye to his ma. He would miss the feisty women who had birthed him 24 years before. But, true to his nature, he didn't linger over sentimental feelings, only acknowledged them and then moved on.

His new farm beckoned. He was ready. His pa's death signaled it was time to make his mark as a man on his own terms and create his own legacy, just as many of his forefathers had done before him.

He turned around in his seat, the joyful moment of the sunrise forgotten. He was about to shout at his wife again when he stopped.

He watched Catherina, with tears in her eyes and her face flushed, hurry to the second wagon with the knotted cloth knapsack that contained their food for today and tomorrow.

His heart softened. He knew she was having a difficult time leaving behind some of the furniture—a couple of pieces he had crafted during the first winter of their marriage—and her fallow garden.

One item being left behind had been her mama's rocker. He couldn't overload the wagons to avoid hurting the animals or slowing down the wagon train, and the costly farm implements had top priority. The farmer was leaving behind plows and other heavy items at the new place. But they would need everything in the wagons for spring planting.

George's demeanor continued to soften as he watched stray pieces of Catherina's dark brown hair escape from the bun at the nape of her neck. He smiled as she tried to keep it contained while hurrying to finish up. She was fastidious, as her mama, Gertrude, had taught her. Gertrude had been a town girl before marrying Papa Henry. Town decorum was different than that of farm girls—many times unreasonably so.

George snapped back to the present when he heard a little voice yell, "Bah!" Maggie, his soon-to-be one-year-old daughter, was waving her small arms in excitement with her tiny bonnet sitting crooked on her head of dark curly hair.

He watched as Papa Henry swung her up in the air for the last time. She squealed with glee as her bonnet flew off her head.

George hoped she would settle down and be too tired to start fussing after they got started. Papa Henry lifted his granddaughter for a final hug and placed her in the second wagon. He told her in a quiet voice, "Now be still and don't upset the horses."

A far-off movement caught his eye. He turned towards the old family home across the field and saw Joshua, his younger brother, pick up their ma. She was now standing on the lower rail of the old wooden fence that surrounded their former horse corral.

Ma was almost five feet tall, a small woman with white hair overshadowing the grey. How she had birthed three sons that were now all six feet tall, he'd never know. She was a tough woman. He knew she would miss each of her sons, but, like all pioneer women, accepted that they had to leave and make their own mark, often never to be seen again.

She waved a white handkerchief high over her head in hopes he could see her.

He took the glove off his left hand to wave back at them. Out of the corner of his eye, he saw Catherina waving too. While they hoped to see one another again, they knew it was unlikely.

He heard a sob. He turned around in time to see tall Papa Henry bend to give tiny Catherina a final hug. He saw Papa Henry thrust a small leather pouch in Catherina's hand. He hoped whatever was in the pouch would provide her comfort. Papa Henry and Uncle Joseph would be missed, especially for the weekly Sunday dinners filled with laughter and catching up on local news.

George continued watching as Papa Henry lifted Catherina up and swung her onto the seat next to Martin Kolb, the man George had hired to drive the second wagon, who then handed Maggie to her.

He sighed again, this time with relief. *Finally!*

As soon as Catherina was seated and ready in the second wagon, George sat up taller to see if the two milk cows were still tethered to their wagon. Then, he did a quick check to see that nothing was hanging over the wooden sides of either wagon. The roads would be rough and rocky at times. It would be difficult and costly, if not impossible, to replace any items damaged en route.

George

The brown and white oxen started mooing, shaking their heads, and stomping their hooves.

It was time! Without hesitation, George slapped the reins on the back of the oxen. With a tug on the harnesses, the oxen stepped forward.

At the same time, Papa Henry gave Maggie a final pat on her head and adjusted her bonnet as their wagon began moving, pulled by two gray workhorses. He gave one last nod to Catherina, who was seated next to the hired man, Martin. He planned to travel west to Kansas where his brother's family had moved ten years after the Civil War. No one in the Kolb family had heard from the brother since.

Martin had agreed to stay with George and Catherina until he saved enough money to go west to see if his brother was still alive. He would be an asset in getting the fields plowed, tilled, and planted this year. Even though Catherina could have driven the wagon herself, she was three months pregnant. George didn't want to exhaust her.

He heard a hard hand slap on the side of his wagon and turned to look down. Papa Henry was walking alongside his moving wagon. George leaned down from the wagon seat and shook hands with the old man, gave him a sad smile and a two-finger salute. Papa Henry nodded. It was their final unspoken goodbye and good luck.

As they made their way down the rutted path to the main road, George watched Joshua walk Ma back to the old family home. Sabrina, their eldest sister, would later pick her up and move her into her family home. After watching them give each other several hugs and goodbyes, their younger brother, Joshua, pulled himself onto his horse. With a final goodbye wave to his ma, he turned and rode his horse out to the main road and turned left. The plan was for him to meet the two wagons where the rutted lane leading to the tenant cabin joined the main road. Together they would travel into Defiance.

Tomorrow morning the brothers would say goodbye for the last time. Joshua would ride north to marry a farm girl named Molly from south Michigan, outside a town called Jackson. He would inherit her pa's farm when the old man died.

As George navigated the ruts of the dirt path that led them to the main road, he was surprised by having second thoughts of leaving.

Deep down he knew it was right to go.

This must have been how Pa and my forefathers felt when each of them left their family homes. Each man hoped that the journey into the unknown provided a better life. But it was also a rite of passage into manhood. Sons that were not firstborn had little to gain by staying. Each one prayed for a better life by leaving.

Many daughters also followed along if there were no men that caused them to stay behind.

I look forward to my own family legacy ... creating a new life built on strong family ties and prosperity.

Many family traditions were set aside, and new ones created during these times, even though many times they resembled the old ones. Regardless, family history did not get left behind. It followed unbidden in the hearts and minds of the descendants, whether rewritten or overlooked, and was replayed throughout future generations.

George and Joshua

George carefully guided the oxen to avoid the ruts and standing water in the lane.

Most of his neighbors and fellow church members in Berlin had told him he was a fool to journey west this time of the year. Well, not in those exact words. But he had understood what they were trying to say. Some had even gone further and told him he should wait until after harvest, or not leave at all.

Yet I'm like my pa. I'm as hardheaded as he was, and I keep my own counsel, too. While I talked these things over with Catherina, once my decision was made it was final. When Pa chose to journey from upper New York state to the upper northwest area of Ohio, Ma came along. They made the best of the challenges that confronted them. Men expected women to abide by their decisions. Right or wrong. Good or bad.

Catherina, Papa Henry, Uncle Joseph, and he had loaded the wagons late yesterday afternoon. They had used old burlap bags to cover the field seed to prevent damage and keep it dry. Next month it would be sown in their new fields. The bags also minimized dust, water, and mud from the road and protected other items. Catherina had a small trunk for her garden seeds, which could be planted in May.

Papa Henry and Uncle Joseph had stayed overnight. In the early morning darkness, they helped hitch the oxen to his wagon and the team of workhorses to the other one. Last week Papa Henry had reinforced the weathered sides of each wagon with newer wood.

They tightened down the wagon covers with rope Catherina had collected during the past four months. This was all done before sunrise. After the early morning meal, Uncle Joseph had said his final goodbye. He had his own livestock and farm to take care of.

He was thankful for the wagon, a wedding gift from his pa. His ma drove over the second wagon after hearing him complain that one wagon wasn't enough. She had said with a wink when she jumped down from the wagon, "Leroy will never miss it." Pa's will did not list every item of property, but it would not have occurred to Leroy to ask for an inventory anyway, since he had no interest in farming.

Although Leroy had moved into town when he turned 18, he was the oldest son and became the sole owner of their pa's farm when he died. The irony was that Leroy seldom helped on the family farm, except during harvest. Even then, he did as little as possible.

Yesterday, only George's ma and Joshua had come for their last meal together. His other siblings had not joined them.

The brothers took their last walk in the field between the two homes. After checking the ropes, George waved at Joshua to join him. Their ma was spending time with her granddaughter, Maggie. Catherina was busy again instructing Papa Henry on how to best take care of himself.

"It'll be interesting to see how long it takes before sparks fly between Ma and Sabrina," Joshua said with a smirk on his face. They both looked over to be sure their ma hadn't overheard him.

George nodded with a grin on his face as they paused. He looked back to watch the old woman fawn over his little girl. Maggie could chatter non-stop.

The Gunther family was patriarchal, like most families in their German Methodist community of Berlin. All decisions were made by the eldest male or landowner for the entire family. Their mother, Mathilde, had taken a couple of steps down in status when her husband, Herman, had died. Her view of how things should be done was no longer relevant. Now, her eldest daughter, Sabrina, and son-in-law would be making all those decisions for her. Ma was expected to abide by them since she would be living in their home.

Originally, Leroy had decreed that Ma should live with Sadie, the youngest. But when Leroy told Sadie the news, Sadie had refused, with her arms crossed and her chin thrust out, reminding him of a willful five-year-old.

Ma and Sadie didn't get along and Ma was unwilling to be part of that family. Sadie had been a belligerent child. To make matters worse, she got pregnant and married at age 15 and kept having children. Ma was unwilling to move with George to an unknown area and leave behind her grandchildren. So, Sabrina stepped up and invited their ma to live with her family, with her husband's permission.

Pa had followed tradition and gave the family farm to Leroy, his eldest son. Leroy had sold the farm, as was his right, after Pa's death.

Everyone knew Ma could not live with Leroy and his family. Leroy's wife was too meek to stand up to Ma and was a town girl. The two of them would have clashed and caused too much chaos and controversy. Ma had always lived on a farm and was very practical and outspoken, not good traits for women who were townspeople.

"What does Leroy plan to do with the money?" Joshua asked George.

"Well, I heard the buyer is waiting for us to leave so he can move in. He plans to marry that Whiteford girl from the farm on the other side of town. He was waiting so there were no hard feelings."

"Would you have bought it if you could?" Joshua asked, believing he already knew the answer.

"I don't know," George responded and shrugged. He looked toward the old two-story farmhouse that had been their home growing up.

So many memories. He snapped his attention back to the conversation, "I would like to think that Leroy would have offered it to me. He knew I wanted it."

"Ja …"

George broke in, "But we both know he would never sell it to me. He didn't want the Gunther family tradition tarnished. If it was mine, and I'm a better farmer, he would have felt shame. His status in town is everything to him. The big important man with money."

They turned and walked back toward the tenant home. Both were careful to bypass any standing water or ice. They then checked for any overlooked items in the corral and the lean-to that housed the animals.

Standing there surveying the old family house and barn from a distance, Joshua said, "Well, I know I didn't want it. I'm looking forward to moving north."

"Ja, Molly is a real pretty girl in her picture, and I hope you will have a good life," George said with emotion in his voice. He slapped his brother on the back, sad that he would not be part of the wedding celebration.

"Thanks. I remember whenever it was chore time, Leroy would disappear," Joshua snickered. The memory was funny now, but they hadn't laughed when they had to finish their chores and Leroy's and feed the animals before they could eat. It was even worse during the harvest, when they also had to unload the hay, grain, or corn.

"Why did pa give it to him?" Joshua said, shaking his head in disbelief. *It wasn't fair or right.*

"Well … I know he had considered giving it to me. But he didn't know how he could do that and give both you and Leroy a share. I told him 90 acres divided by three was too small for me. I want a large place," George replied. "One I can grow and expand."

He remembered the several conversations he had had with his pa about the farm. Last August was the last time. They were boarding up the north side of the corral where the cows had kicked a hole through the rotting wood. A couple of weeks later Pa died when a bale of hay toppled over, suffocating him beneath it.

George thought, *I wished I would have insisted he do the right thing instead of talking about it.*

"Do you think his German heritage made the decision for him?" Joshua asked. He remembered the stories Pa and Ma told them at the dinner table and how family traditions fascinated him. How Pa had resented having to leave Germany and travel to America. He'd made the journey after his oldest brother had inherited the family farm.

"Pa still believed the eldest son should inherit the farm since it was a tradition," Joshua commented as he petted the wet noses of the oxen after feeding them.

"Also, he wanted others in the community and church to think well of him," George replied thoughtfully. "It mattered to him. German pride dictated handing down his farm to his eldest son, so his sweat and toil had meaning."

"Ja," Joshua said. He shook his head, thinking, *family.* He helped George finish checking the oxen and workhorses to ensure they had feed and water for the evening.

"What would you have done if he had handed it down to you instead of Leroy?" Joshua asked again. He asked as the dinner bell clanged, announcing supper—their last meal together.

"Well, we'll never know. Pa wasn't a person to follow through on his convictions if it ran against the traditional way of doing things," George replied.

He remembered his pa had been on the fence about what to do since Leroy had no intention of being a farmer. His father had prayed that Leroy would change his mind once the farm was his.

George had shaken his head in disbelief at his father's denial. But it hadn't been George's decision to make in the end. Now, he was doing what he needed to do for himself.

"Pa attempted to break tradition when he left stipends for Ma and each of us, including our sisters," Joshua said as they skirted around a large patch of ice along the north fence of the corral.

"Well, as you know, Leroy hates farming. He hates getting dirty. He doesn't have the patience for it. His pride wouldn't consider giving it or selling it to either of us. Especially if he knew how much we wanted it," George said as they paused at the door into the tenant home. They inhaled the smells of dinner as they washed up.

He'd been careful not to tell Joshua that it would have meant a lot to have the farm and be able to buy it.

I don't want to hurt Joshua's feelings. But I deserved the farm since I worked the hardest and stayed the longest. But I won't say that to anyone. I love my brothers and sisters, George thought to himself.

"I hope it works out for Leroy and our sisters' families. I hope things work out for you in your new place. If I can, I'll visit you next year," Joshua said. Then he bent down to tickle Maggie, who had crawled over to them. He swung her up with care so she didn't hit her head on the low ceiling as they walked to the dinner table. She giggled gleefully at her uncle's attention.

Joshua and George

Immediately after the meal, Joshua tilted his head to his ma. It was time for them to leave.

"It's too bad all the family couldn't get together one last time," he said to George. "I'll see you in the morning." George nodded.

They were waiting for Ma to finish hugging Catherina and Maggie goodbye. Ma nodded to Papa Henry as Uncle Joseph swung her up on the buggy seat.

"Sabrina agreed. But she and Sadie couldn't do anything to make it happen. Their husbands were afraid of any retribution and gossip that Leroy and his wife might cause. Everyone wants to continue living here without any problems," Joshua shared.

"Ja … community and church acceptance are more important than family. Yet, they say, family is the blood of life." George said, shaking his head.

Joshua sat squirming in his saddle. His horse was also ready to go. But courtesy demanded he wait and have their ma leave first.

He turned when Maggie yelled "Bah!" Ma started crying after one last look at the little girl, knowing that she would miss watching her growing up. Joshua gave a finger wave to hide his own tears. He would miss watching her grow up too and hoped to have his own children in the future.

George sighed, watching his ma shed tears and Joshua struggle to prevent his own, while tipping his hat down. When Ma finally flicked the reins, the buggy moved. Joshua dug his heels into the side of his horse to follow and prayed she wouldn't sob all the way back. He never knew how to handle crying women, particularly since his ma was usually the strong one.

George hung his head in sadness as he walked toward the cabin door. He wished all his family could have been here. It didn't matter that his sisters and brothers and their family wouldn't see each other again. No one thought of regrets. They blamed Joshua and him for not wanting to live in their community any longer.

Even though the family had worked hard together to create the family farm, patriarchal tradition broke apart families when they could no longer live together.

Then, George snickered. Joshua seemed in a hurry to leave right after the meal. He bet Joshua feared Catherina bossing him around with more chores. Since she was a hard worker, she believed everyone should do the same. George sighed as she and Maggie waited for him in the doorway. He hoped that her list wasn't much longer.

George

After Joshua joined them on the main road into town, he rode alongside the second wagon. He had tied his second horse, which carried his personal effects, including a wedding gift from his ma, George, and their sisters, to the second wagon.

George thought again of Leroy as they plodded along with the oxen leading the way. They seemed to know where they were going.

The two brothers had nodded when George went to the general store a couple days ago to settle his accounts. Leroy happened to be there at the same time; otherwise, there would not have been a final goodbye.

Leroy tipped his new black felt hat toward George when he was ready to leave the store. George extended his hand and both brothers shook hands without a word.

After Leroy had gone, the storekeeper spoke in a soft voice. "Did you know your brother is building a fancy home? He's also building a new mill about a half-mile outside of town by the river."

George had shrugged and didn't respond. With a sad smile, he finished paying the man and left. *No, he hadn't known.*

George didn't like the fact that Leroy received a windfall of money from the sale of the farm to do with as he pleased. But he was thankful Leroy had given each of them the stipends listed in the will. He knew that other families had not been so lucky when the head of the family died. Leroy had even paid

Joshua and him each a third after the final harvest last fall. Of course, the two brothers had each done half the work.

George knew Leroy would gloat about his generosity to the church and townspeople. Leroy expected respect for his good deeds. But there was nothing George could do about the hypocrisy. In his no-nonsense way, he shrugged away the memory. *Nothing to be gained by thinking more about it.*

George turned his thoughts to Catherina. They had married two years before on July 4th when she was 18 and he was 22. They had grown up on adjoining farms, with the property line marked by rocks. Like others in the community, they had attended the one-room school. He and his brothers attended after fall harvest and before spring planting. He had courted her a couple of times before he talked to her about marriage.

But to be honest, it was Minister Herzer of their German Methodist church who encouraged the union. They did like one another. But he had taken a fancy to another girl on the other side of town until he heard her tell a church member that she wanted to move into Defiance and get away from the village of Berlin once she was married. That wasn't acceptable to him. He had planned to build his dream … a big farm … a legacy … a large family to call his own.

His primary hesitation about Catherina was concern over her ability to have children since she was only 5' 3" and small-boned. Minister Herzer had grinned and waved away the excuse. He stated with a grin, "I've never seen a harder worker. She's also good with numbers, writing, and reading. I believe she'll be the one you need to marry."

Then, the minister had reminded George that he was expected to settle down soon and start his family, as was the tradition in their community.

George had wanted to wait until he had his own place, but it hadn't worked out that way. It turned out to be a blessing since Catherina was a hard worker. It never ceased to amaze him how his wife could get so much done, especially when it came to her "little field." He planned to create another one for her once they arrived.

A couple of times he had surprised himself by saying to her, "Slow down … enjoy the moment."

She had replied with a half-smile, "I will when I'm old and gray … until then, I've a lot to do."

He felt blessed with his little girl and another kid on the way. This time he hoped for a boy. He knew he'd need many of them to expand the farm he'd bought.

George – March 1, 1886

George learned that Catherina rarely showed emotion. But she hadn't been able to hide her feelings about leaving behind her Papa Henry and uncle Joseph. They would now have to survive without family nearby. She had wanted them to come with them, at times begging them to rethink it. But both had said no … they would be fine and take care of each other.

Catherina's ma, Gertrude, had passed in 1883, along with her two younger sisters. As the eldest surviving daughter, it became her responsibility to take care of her Papa Henry and her two younger brothers. But both brothers left home when the oldest one turned 16 and the younger one was not yet 15. They hated living on a farm and all the extra farm chores they now had to do after their younger sisters passed away. They didn't visit Papa Henry or their sister after they left.

There had been several family conversations about the two boys needing to come home and take over the two Schoenly farms. George didn't understand why they would work so hard for someone else with nothing to show for it. He believed they only received a pittance in wages, while sleeping in a bunkhouse. It was not a life filled with hope or wealth. As a farmer, the money was in the property, but it was something that was yours. He kept his thoughts to himself. His opinions would make no difference and only add to the hurt Papa Henry and Uncle Joseph felt.

They'll be fine, George thought. Catherina forgot that her Papa Henry and uncle Joseph had left Pennsylvania to build homesteads in Ohio. They had survived and would continue to do so.

He knew she would miss the two old men. He would too. But hoped she would embrace their new community once they got there. He believed there was too much work to do to miss anyone.

As the procession moved closer to Defiance and he waved at a farmer herding his cattle, George was surprised to feel tears sting his eyes. They were leaving behind the only life they had known. There would have been nothing gained by staying. He doubted he would ever return. He also knew he was moving his family into the unknown. But he had the faith it would all work out. He believed his family would prosper and leave a great family legacy.

He understood a man's pride was leaving his family wealthy. Like his forefathers before him, he needed to honor his pride and make his mark in this life. His pa had done well, and he expected to do better.

His own parents had emigrated from Germany to the United States. They had each left when their eldest brothers inherited the family farms in Germany. When they first arrived, his parents had settled in upper New York state, then moved with a group of Germans to northwest Ohio. They wanted their own farms with fertile soil. The group built a German Methodist church in which to worship, and the village of Berlin was born and branched out to encompass it. Many never saw their parents or siblings again. It was a common story for many pioneers throughout history. His pa had worked work hard and had done well enough but had lost track of the two brothers who had come to America with him.

He vowed as they moved closer to Defiance to have the courage to do the right thing for his own sons. He prayed he would not be saddled by tradition when it came time to bequeath his farm. He would give it to the son who deserved it the most.

He said a silent prayer, *please give me the courage to not have my family legacy be a curse on my family. I want no regrets when I die.*

He never again thought about the old leather pouch Papa Henry had thrust into Catherina's hands. Unbeknownst to him, this seemingly insignificant event would resurface decades later and impact his family's legacy.

Catherina – March 1, 1886

Catherina rocked with the swaying of the wagon as it moved down the rutted lane to the main road. Her worse fears had come true. She kept her eyes looking down at her chapped hands in her lap. She curled in on herself for comfort. Occasionally, she felt a small hand pat her lap and heard a little voice ask, "Mama?"

She ignored it, stifled a sob, and hoped the bonnet she had donned after being seated in the wagon hid any tears.

Papa Henry had promised to take her mama's rocker and keep it safe until they saw one another again. She prayed he would do so. But like so many women before her, she knew it was unlikely she would see her beloved papa again … or the old wooden rocker.

There had been hope that George would have ownership of the Gunther farm after Papa Gunther passed. The hope included Papa Henry adding his acreage to it, and Uncle Joseph's 20 acres too. It would have kept them all together as a family. She could have kept her little field and expanded it.

But Leroy was only concerned about Leroy and elevating his status among the people living in the village as it grew into a town. When he sold the Gunther farm without notice, they had no choice but to move away from the community.

She sighed, devastated by the impact one man's decision had on the lives of so many people, but she refused to allow any more tears to flow. Life dictated that she was to follow her husband's lead wherever he traveled.

At the end of the rutted lane, Martin asked in a soft voice, "Do you want a moment to look back?"

She shook her head and continued to ignore the little hand patting her lap.

After a mile down the road, reality set in. It was final.

With inner acceptance, she inhaled and felt her spine straighten. The old leather pouch that she had been kneading in her hands became still. Her fingers slowly made out the contents. It hadn't occurred to her to open it. Instead, she calculated the best place to hide it for safekeeping.

When Maggie started crying again, she shushed her, while glancing at Martin. He only glanced back at her with his face expressionless and returned to watching the road ahead.

Maggie patted her lap again, this time harder. "Mama? Mama?" Her chant had become insistent.

Catherina patted Maggie's shoulder and adjusted her little bonnet.

She leaned down and whispered in her ear, "Mama good."

Out of the corner of her eye she caught Joshua watching her. She sat up tall before turning to look him straight in the eye. He gave her a slight nod, which she returned. Her determination to make the best of it had returned.

A few minutes later, she saw that Joshua was riding alongside the wagon. He asked, "Do you want Maggie to ride with me?"

She nodded. Martin stopped the horse team and she handed Maggie over the side rail of the wooden bench seat. At first Maggie was agitated, but after Joshua started singing her a German lullaby, she settled. They resumed their journey.

The cool air and frost disappeared as the sun rose higher. It lifted her spirits. She opened her palm to catch droplets of melted snow from the branches that hung over the road. With her eyes focused straight ahead, she felt the turn of the wagon wheels.

With each step the oxen and horses took, her dreams of being a farmer evaporated. The wagons plodded on and everyone was silent in their own thoughts. Maggie had stopped making noises and fell asleep nestled up against her uncle Joshua on his horse.

Catherina prayed George's dream of owning a big farm and bestowing a prosperous family legacy for future generations was enough for both of them. The seed collection from her little field was safely tucked away in a trunk. The tiny specks of life would grow strong in the Illinois soil and sun and nourish the little one growing within her. Her future children too, bequeathing to them a bigger legacy than if they had stayed in Ohio.

Fond and sad memories of the life on Papa Henry's northwest Ohio farm would always remain etched in her heart.

A new life awaited and she was finally ready to accept it. She prayed there would be no regrets.

PART 2

Seeds of hope are planted each year,
and with any luck, harvested too.

Matthew – November 11, 1927

Matthew, George's and Catherina's second youngest son, stood at the side door of his parents' home scraping muck off the bottom of his large work boots. He knocked twice before opening the old wooden door and closing it fast to keep out the cold. He opened his long work coat, exposing his blue flannel work shirt, and stripped off his work gloves to feel the warmth from the fireplace.

The first thing he noticed as he looked around the living and kitchen areas was everything looked clean and neat. So, he thrust the gloves in his coat pockets instead of placing them on the clean kitchen trestle table. Then removed his work boots and set them back outside. He couldn't remember a time when everything looked so nice.

It was then he noticed his ma standing in the doorway to his parent's bedroom with the kerosene lamp shining in the background. He gave her a questioning look. She smiled in reply and beckoned him in with a nod.

His parents had sent him a note earlier in the day asking him to visit when it was his turn to help his second oldest brother, Peter, with the daily chores. Now the animals' stalls were cleaned and bedded with fresh straw and supplied with fresh water and food. He wondered why his brothers and he had to help Peter care for these animals. It wasn't hard work, nor time-consuming.

It was why his brothers had given Peter the nickname Leroy, after their famously lazy uncle. But his brothers showed unity by staying quiet in hopes of not becoming the victim of Peter's ire and gossip.

It was a cold and cloudless late afternoon, but not a bitterly cold day like the Novembers had been in recent years. He was anxious to learn what his parents needed from him. He wanted to get back home for his oldest daughter's ninth birthday dinner before the sun set. His wife and daughters were waiting on him.

Matthew hoped his visit would be short and he would not be regaled with a long-winded story from long ago.

Catherina – September 1927

In June 1927, two years before the official start of the Great Depression in 1929, George suffered a second stroke. His first one had been in March of that year. He was with four of his five sons planting corn in the west field. This time the stroke left him paralyzed on his left side.

While three of his sons moved him into the house and into his bed, Peter jumped onto one of the workhorses to fetch the town doctor. He believed it would be faster than cranking up his pa's Model T.

Two months later, their third oldest son Benjamin made a rare visit to the house. He was busy from sunup to sundown working on his father-in-law's farm on the other side of Harrison and also was married and had young children.

Catherina stood next to the bedroom door instructing the neighbor girl on the right way to carry the bedpan outdoors. Yesterday, she'd instructed the girl, "Push the dirt out the door. Don't bat at it." It seemed like she had to remind the girl every day how to do things.

Catherina watched with forced calm as the girl moved hesitantly toward the outside door, praying nothing would slop on the clean floor.

As she turned to go into the kitchen to address the next item on her mental checklist, she overheard George say to Benjamin, "Unfortunately, I lived." Earlier in the day he'd received the horrible news from the town doctor that he would be confined to his bed for the rest of his life because of a third stroke earlier in the week.

She stopped. Then, took a few steps backward to the doorway to listen. But he had nothing more to say. It saddened her, but she understood. All George could do was lie there day after day until he gained back some of his strength. Physically, he would never be the same active man he once was.

George was outgoing and had an upbeat smile for each visitor. He dearly loved talking with each of his seven children and multiple grandchildren when they came to see him. He enjoyed being everyone's favorite and relished the attention. When the old-timers from the area would come for a visit or a game of chess, the old men would laugh about the old stories, retelling them over and over. Even Catherina had to grin at the noisy laughter. It did her heart good to hear George laugh just as loud.

Her hope was that the doctor was wrong in this diagnosis. But she was prepared to do her duty as George's wife and care for him. She felt deep sadness that George would never again be the robust man she had married.

She knew George could be obstinate. She would give him a half-smile and threaten to tell everyone what he was really like if he didn't do his bed exercises and eat certain foods. He'd comply with a sly grin on his face. His reputation for being a successful, well-liked farmer was important to him as the patriarch of one of the important old families in the Harrison area.

Peter – October 1927

Peter and his family moved into the tenant home about a half-mile away from the farmhouse in July 1927. He had lost his own farm after a heavy rainstorm in June wiped out the corn crop he'd planted. The bank threatened to foreclose since he'd already had three years of crop failures in a row and was behind in his mortgage payments. He felt he'd outsmarted the bank by selling the farm before they could foreclose, even though it left only a few dollars in his pocket.

Peter dubbed himself the overseer of the Gunther & Sons farm and insisted each of his brothers step up and help him. In his mind, his job was to ensure his brothers helped him daily milk the cows, care for the workhorses, clean the stalls, and harvest the corn and wheat crops. And, help their ma care for their pa.

Each brother was assigned a day when he was expected to help. One of Peter's brothers would arrive mid-afternoon and do the chores Peter assigned.

Peter rationalized he was doing his parents and siblings a favor by managing the farm for them—a huge responsibility.

He had an agreement with his parents that he wouldn't pay any expenses since he had no money but would split the profits 50/50 with them. It was a verbal agreement sealed by a handshake between George and Peter.

He believed overseeing the property was doing his share of the work, even though his brothers often made remarks about him being able to do more. He'd shrug and say nothing. He took his responsibility seriously.

Peter's brothers complained amongst themselves about who was doing more than his share. Three of them had their own farms to work.

But their German heritage taught them to honor their parents, so it didn't occur to any of them not to help.

Peter knew his brothers had nicknamed him "Leroy" after the uncle they had never met. His pa had entertained them with stories for most of their lives about his lazy brother. Peter believed he was destined for more and wasn't lazy. It was just that life didn't help him become rich like Leroy.

During the first week of October, he devised a plan to help his parents overcome any financial woes and shared it with his brothers. George and Catharina would sell their farm to all five sons. With the money George and Catherina received, they would in turn give $1,000 to each of their sons. In return, each son would pay annual interest back to their parents. The interest would be a type of retirement fund for their parents. But after his oldest sister, Maggie, heard about it, she demanded that he expand the plan to include the two sisters, all seven children, or risk her tongue-lashing.

In Peter's head, his plan included continuing to live in the tenant's home and fixing it up. He would live there with his wife and two sons until his parents both passed away. Then, he would sell it and move into the family farmhouse as the patriarch.

George had purchased the old tenant home and acreage from a former neighbor, Isaac Archenbronn. George had given Isaac cash and wished him the best on the man's quest to find his fortune in gold in the Rocky Mountains of Colorado.

George mocked these types of farmers and gold-diggers to his family, saying, "You still need to work the land to prosper and find what you are seeking. A farm is made up of dirt. It's what we do with it that creates a man's worth."

Peter remembered his pa saying to him and his brothers, "Not all farmers are meant to be farmers." George was proud that all his sons were farm owners, except for Matthew.

Matthew had taken a year to work on the railroad before marrying Grace and becoming a tenant farmer on the Smythe farm nearby. The family silently hoped Matthew would find his way and buy his own farm too. Even though he'd registered for the WWI draft as required, he was never called.

George and Catherina helped each of their sons get started by providing a small amount of money *when* they purchased their first farms. Maggie and Rachel also received the same small amount after Maggie demanded equal treatment. Matthew hadn't received his money from his parents yet and wouldn't until he bought a farm.

But Peter's siblings found his plan unacceptable. While the $1,000 would be a godsend, they would never know from year to year if they could pay the interest. Like many farmers, there were years each of them experienced a boon and other years when every penny was counted to survive. They refused to owe money so no one could call them thieves.

No one voiced their true thoughts about Peter's idea. They feared the gossip Peter would spew about them. He always did this when he was upset. Peter was brash and combative, and known to hold a grudge. Rejecting one of his ideas, especially one this big, would guarantee his wrath. They were willing to wait for their inheritance of prime farmland when their pa and ma passed.

But Maggie wasn't shy. When Peter stopped in her general store to buy sugar for his wife's canning, she told him, "We'll not be following your plan."

Predictably, Peter became angry and stormed out of the general store, slamming the door behind him and leaving a couple other customers gawking. He expected his siblings to do it his way; after all, he'd given it a lot of thought.

After walking around town muttering to himself about his stupid siblings, he stopped to talk with a couple of old-timers sitting in their rockers in front of the local diner. He overheard them mentioning a farmer needing help and asked them to tell him more.

So, five days later in a defiant tone, he proudly announced to George he was leaving as overseer of the Gunther & Sons farm. He'd found a way to buy his own farm, mostly with the money he'd received from the crop sales. He'd struck a deal with the farmer to give him a fourth of the payment for the corn crop after it was harvested since he wanted to be seen as the good guy in town. A roving harvesting group had already committed to Peter to harvest the crop for a fourth of the profit. He was happy he'd be left with the other half of the profits.

He felt triumphant he had again outsmarted the bank by paying the farmer a monthly sum for the farm.

There would be enough profits to tide him and his family over for the next year. His new farm was twenty miles south of Harrison, far enough away so he wouldn't be expected to pitch in when hands were needed.

His goal was to show his family he was smarter than the rest of them and he didn't need them to prosper.

George – November 10, 1927

After enjoying a rare Indian summer day that was turning into a cold evening with the promise of a hard freeze, Catherina rocked while darning one of George's wool socks. George lay in bed with pillows plumped up behind his head and shoulders. They listened to the news on the radio about the food lines starting to grow longer each day. They feared what it would mean for their family and the families in the Harrison area in the future.

The radio commentator painted a picture of gloom and doom, predicting banks would close their doors and people would lose their homes. They shook their head at the travesty. But George wasn't worried. He kept his money hidden in the farmhouse and their mortgage had been paid in full last year.

What worried them was the need for someone to manage the Gunther & Sons farm. Their money wouldn't last forever, and their reputation demanded it.

"Now what are we going to do? Peter won't be living here and managing the farm, so we're left without help," George complained to Catherina. It was two weeks before Thanksgiving and a big celebration was planned for the family. The cooking and baking had already begun spicing the air.

He had overheard his sons complaining about Peter's laziness and understood their dilemma. The extra work they incurred during these past months couldn't continue since each of them had their own farms. He'd heard about Peter's plan and why it backfired on him. He also understood Peter's wanting to save his pride and show everyone he was as good as the rest of them.

George and Catherina reminisced about raising their seven living children. They still felt a sense of sadness for their first son, Henry Joseph, who had passed away two days after he was born on August 16, 1886. They blamed the long wagon ride since the journey had lasted three weeks instead of the promised two. They still arrived in late March with several weeks to wait before planting season would begin.

They both felt the pride of ownership. Between 1886 and 1927, they had expanded their farm from 200 acres to 500 acres, beyond their dreams. They became known by the good townspeople of Harrison to be prosperous, hard-working, and faithful. Many appreciated their generosity. When farmers came to George wanting him to buy them out, George gave them a fair price if he was interested. It was one of the ways he expanded his acreage without the back-breaking work of clearing more farmland.

Before this devastating year, George had relied upon his sons, grandsons, and seasonal help. Now he was at a loss for what to do with Peter leaving.

After a few minutes of silence, Catherina turned to look at George and said, "Each of our sons has his own farm. We don't have any sons-in-law. That makes it difficult for us to rely upon them and their families to take care of this farm too. We could move into town, but this is our home. We built it and raised our family here."

They sat silently watching the flames from the fireplace. Catherina added wood to get them through the night, then sat back down in her rocker.

"What about Matthew?" George asked. Maggie had suggested this to him two days ago when she had visited and brought them food staples from her general store. She had told him that her siblings were not interested in Peter's scheme.

George asked, "What should I do?"

Maggie had replied in a demeaning tone, "Matthew isn't doing anything."

George explored her idea further. "He doesn't own a farm. He's a tenant farmer on the old Smythe farm down the road, hoping to save enough money to buy his own farm. He could move here with his family and farm this one. He doesn't have the money to buy his own farm, or enough horses and farm tools yet. Even with the small gift of money we give to each of our sons, it wouldn't be enough today to get him started with farm prices the way they are right now. We have the things he needs. The land here is much better. We could give him his money now and he could save it for the lean years."

Maggie had nodded with a slight smile. Her pa continued thinking it over long after Maggie had returned to town, where she lived with her son, Nathaniel.

When George told Catherina about his conversation with Maggie, both thought about the times George had driven Catherina to see Matthew and his family. George had loved showing off his Ford Model T. He'd give his granddaughters pennies for their piggy banks. Emma, Matthew's second-oldest, was the only one who saved each penny.

Each time, they were depressed to see Matthew living as a tenant farmer and giving away his profits to someone else. They believed his family was unhappy being poor too.

Now, maybe they could do something about it.

It was turning cold the following late afternoon of November 11th after they'd eaten an early dinner. The farmhouse offered tantalizing smells of ginger and cinnamon from all the baking earlier in the day. They'd settled in for the night even though the sun had not set yet. They listened to the radio in growing apprehension about the food lines in several cities.

They heard a double knock at the door. Before Catherina could get out of the rocker, Matthew had opened the door and closed it as fast as he could against the cold. Catherina had sent him a message via one of the neighborhood boys needing a coin for his family to buy food.

He pulled one of the wooden chairs into the bedroom where his parents were and sat down close to them. He nodded as he listened to their concerns about the future of the Gunther & Sons farm. Then, was surprised they wanted him and his family to move back and work it.

They talked about a 50/50 split of expenses for seed, feed, and breeding stock. George thought it should be more, given the work he'd be expected to do. But they also knew it was a better deal than the third Matthew currently was being given.

But due to Peter's recent behavior, Catherina insisted that it should be kept at 50/50. She wanted to restore family unity.

It was what they had paid Peter, but George failed to factor in that Peter didn't pay the expenses, he only reaped the profits. When Catherina, who took care of the financial books, attempted to speak up, George shushed her. He'd reached his decision.

After a few minutes of silence, George told Matthew, "Since everyone else already has their own farm, you can have this one after we're both gone."

Stunned, both Catherina and Matthew looked at George.

Matthew looked back and forth from Catherina and George to ensure he'd heard right. Both nodded.

Then, Matthew stood and thanked his pa for his generosity, while leaning down to shake his hand, sealing the agreement.

"No talk of this with the others. Let's wait for the right time to tell them. This situation with Peter is still too upsetting for everyone," George decreed.

Then Matthew went to leave, saying, "I need to get home to celebrate Susan's birthday."

"Wait a minute," Catherina said.

She moved from her rocker with normal swiftness when focused on a duty. She came back into the bedroom with a wrapped book, a gift for Matthew to give her granddaughter, a voracious reader.

Fifteen minutes later, after Matthew had brought in more firewood and stoked the fire for the evening, he rode his horse home with a gift much larger than the book safely tucked inside his heavy barn coat. It was a dream come true.

The Gunther family name was as important as the size of their farm in the community. Both his parents and he wanted

Gunther & Sons, painted in white bold letters on the red barn, to mean something

No one put the agreement into writing. They were family and didn't need to do so. Their word was their promise.

Unspoken also was the promise that Catherina would honor her husband's agreement, whether he was alive or not, whether she agreed or not, and regardless of whether others thought it was the right thing to do.

Matthew and Peter – November 13, 1927

It was a sunny cold day two days later. The winds had finally calmed down and the weather turned warmer than in the past few days. The dry blowing snow that had been stuck in the ruts and ditches had melted.

Matthew and his wife Grace, and their three daughters, Susan, Emma, and Paulina, moved into the tenant's home on the Gunther farm. They didn't have a lot to bring. Matthew had told Grace about the handshake and promise of the Gunther & Sons farm becoming theirs in the future. It was their secret.

The day before their move, Peter had taken the Gunther wagon and the team of horses to move his family out. They hadn't had a lot to move either, but they took the better furniture that had been part of the tenant home, claiming it as their own.

No one spoke a word as the two brothers silently exchanged the same wagon and team of horses for Matthew's move. Neither helped the other since Peter was still seething over his siblings not seeing the value of his plan. All the siblings stayed away, not wanting to take sides.

The following day after both brothers had moved, Peter showed up with his sons to claim his livestock. Matthew and he became further estranged when Peter insisted that he had a right to the younger animals since he had lived there when they were born.

He hadn't paid for them or paid for their feed but had helped birth a calf and two sets of piglets when the cow and two sows needed help. Peter believed that his parents would never know which animals he took. Catherina did not come out to the barns and trusted her sons to do right by them.

Matthew, an honest man, couldn't agree to any deception. It wasn't in his nature. George and Catherina agreed with Matthew. The animals were theirs. If Peter wanted to take a male and female to breed, he could have a pair. But the final straw for Peter was when Matthew told him that a young sow he wanted couldn't have piglets.

"But it's mine," Peter exclaimed, throwing his hands up in frustration.

"Why do you have to be so difficult?" Peter yelled, glaring at his younger brother. His two sons cowered in a stall with a pony.

"Then take it," Matthew said, looking Peter directly in the eye. "But don't say I didn't warn you."

Catherina came running outside after she heard Peter yelling. She repeated what Matthew had said. "She can't have piglets. But if you really want her, take her. Just stop the yelling. It's upsetting your pa."

The following year when Peter tried to breed the sow, he was unsuccessful. He blamed Matthew for cheating him. It made him even angrier when he had to spend his own money to buy a sow to breed.

The two brothers never spoke to one another again.

The following year when Jacob mentioned to his parents that Peter was still angry at Matthew over the incident, they shook their heads in denial. They appreciated Matthew's honesty about the livestock, but felt Jacob was overreacting about Peter making such a big deal about a sow. After all, Peter had bought a prize sow from a farmer and had been boasting about it when he visited.

But George got angry after listening to Jacob, which was unusual, and exclaimed, "It's just a pig! Enough! It's done!" Then he had a coughing spell that had Catherina glaring at him. Jacob warned his siblings to never speak about the incident again.

But Peter was not going to be quiet about what Matthew had done. Over the past year, Matthew had gained a good reputation as a hard worker and had a gift for training horses. Other farmers were starting to respect George's second youngest son. It irked Peter since he believed he was losing his status as a successful older son after leaving as overseer of the Gunther & Sons farm.

Peter continued his gossip to anyone who would listen. In his mind, he had worked hard to keep his parents' farm in operation that first year after George's stroke. He failed to mention his brothers being required to show up daily to do the work or how he personally profited.

Since George and Catherina were homebound, they didn't hear Peter's stories. Not that they could have done anything about it. When family members or neighbors visited, they were careful not to mention the problems Peter was having with Matthew or to share the stories he told.

But when grandchildren visited, they were not as careful and were shushed. Once they got home, they were punished for talking about something they shouldn't talk about. The hypocrisy confused the grandchildren of all ages since they knew Uncle Peter told a lot of stories. What they didn't question was the truth of these stories. Instead, they used them to taunt Matthew's daughters, their cousins, about being freeloaders and scrounging off their grandparents. They remembered many of these stories and believed in Matthew's sins for the rest of their lives.

At first, Peter gained sympathy for all the sacrifices he'd made. Then the truth about Peter losing his first farm forced him to change his story. The new story was about having to sell his first farm at a loss to support his ma and invalid pa. After all, they were too old to handle it themselves.

But as one wise old-timer commented to Maggie, "If your brother spent his time farming instead of telling so many stories about his brother, he might become a success."

While the siblings and their families were angry that Peter was milking the situation for his benefit, they sought a united family front by saying nothing. Yes, they were concerned about the wrong done by Matthew to Peter, according to Peter. But no one asked for the facts, and Matthew was too easy-going and peace-loving to confront Peter. The truth was, as long as Peter focused his anger on Matthew, they felt safe from Peter turning his anger on them.

Peter's stories became part of the folklore of the family and were retold for generations as the truth.

Five years later, Peter sold what was left of his struggling farm when both of his sons moved to Detroit, Michigan to work in a factory. He paid the farmer what was left of the property note. Then Peter and his wife joined their sons in Michigan. Peter got a job working on the line for a carmaker, eventually becoming a union organizer due to his gift of gab and harsh criticisms of management.

Yet, until the day he died, he blamed Matthew for the loss of his second farm too. He was angry he'd been forced to move away from Harrison, where his last name meant something and made him feel important.

Matthew – 1927 to 1939

Matthew was the quiet one in his family and had trouble at times getting his words out. He wasn't the type to talk about others or feel the need to defend himself. He focused his attention and stayed busy working the farm for his parents and his future, doing so without complaint. Each year he felt in his bones the pride of owning land and building a legacy— supporting his pa's dreams … and his own dreams too.

Every year he removed stumps and rocks to clear more land to increase the number of bushels of corn, oats, wheat, and soybeans they sold. He also expanded the field of alfalfa to increase bales of hay to feed livestock and sell to other farmers.

These hours of working the fields were long. But Matthew was out there during the spring, summer, and fall to ensure all was well. He hired seasonal labor. His brothers and their sons helped as needed since it was their father's and grand-father's farm. Each man had visions of someday being the owner of the 500-acre farm. Crop prices were just adequate due to the significant price drop because of the Great Depression.

His brothers and sisters-in-law silently rejoiced that Matthew was helping their parents. It took the burden off them. They could concentrate on their own farms. But they did express concerns amongst themselves about Matthew freeloading off his parents; after all, he had been a tenant and not a farm owner. This was a big step up, overseeing a much larger farm. Peter's continuing gossip about his being gypped only added fuel to their concerns.

Matthew's wife, Grace, stood 5'6." She was strong and large-boned, with prematurely gray hair and a beautiful smile that shone upon others. She had a high school diploma and loved school. But her pa refused to let her become the teacher she wanted to be. Instead, before marrying, she wrote stories to share with her family. Now she kept these hidden in a box under the bed since she didn't have the time and energy to write.

She was well organized after learning domestic skills from a very young age from her Mama Leota and Grandma Mabel. She fed and clothed her family and kept the tenant home clean. But there was a lot to do, including handling the money and bookkeeping to ensure their accounts matched Catherina's. Behind the tenant home, she grew a large vegetable garden with an array of items for canning each year. She also managed the fruit tree orchard in the back of the farm for both families since Catherina could no longer keep up the huge one-acre garden and handle the work in the orchard too, as she was once famous for.

Matthew and Grace always felt better when they received their annual monies. One year they received extra money from selling red wheat, a heartier version of the traditional white wheat sold by many neighboring farmers. Matthew had recommended it. George and Catherina had agreed. Both profited. In the following years, other farmers followed suit and Matthew's reputation continued to improve.

While Matthew and his family were poor by their family's standards, they survived. The monies they received took care of their basic needs. A little was left to put away in a hidden canning jar that served as their savings account.

George and Catherina did well enough from Matthew's family's efforts. Matthew saw Jacob and Charlie, who had farms close by, during harvest, and he saw them at family get-togethers. Matthew took care of the daily chores of feeding the animals, with help from his daughters. Catherina and George had no complaints and felt Matthew was very easy to work with. The brothers and families were happy they didn't have to deal with Catherina's demands for how things should be done. It seemed as though Matthew and she got along well.

But one thing that couldn't be overlooked by Matthew and Grace was when Catherina gave money to local farm girls to help with household chores. She was always very kind to them. The story her cousins told at school was that their granddaughters had refused to help her.

In fact, Matthew's daughters were willing to do their share. But when Grace reminded them that it was their turn to help their grandparents, they complained their kind grandma wasn't so kind to them.

Grace would say, "Just be nice. Do what she tells you and don't talk back at her."

Then, one day one of the farm girls at school mentioned the money Catherina gave to help her family.

Grace's daughters put smiles on their faces and told Grace about it.

Grace and Matthew decided that they needed to maintain the peace. Their future was not going to be derailed by this situation. George still had not put his promise in writing. So, the required pail of milk and basket of eggs still had to be delivered each morning before Susan, Emma, and Paulina went to school. But helping their grandma with household chores would be limited to special situations. They would still be expected to visit and smile when visiting their grandparents on Sundays along with the rest of the Gunther family.

While they were doing better than many of their neighbors, they didn't have extra money as the community liked to believe about George and Catherina. The truth was their wealth—like that of many farmers—was tied up in the value of their land, and not in the amount hidden in their mattress or sitting in the local bank.

Matthew's survival and financial success depended on the weather and crop sales. Each year they put in their money to pay for 50 percent of the seed. They were debt-free.

Matthew and his family knew they were more fortunate than others. Most of their food was grown in their garden. During the Great Depression, they used food coupons for basic staples like sugar, just like everyone else in their area. For example, they bartered with other farmers for squash and other items in exchange for apples from their fruit trees in the fall.

They canned fruit and vegetables over the summer. Cabbage was packed into crocks to make sauerkraut. Peaches, cucumbers, and beans were pickled and canned. Each fall a cow and pig were slaughtered for meat. In early spring, they made maple syrup and sold it. In the fall they gathered walnuts and hickory nuts. No one in the family went hungry. They shared their provisions with Catherina and George.

Grace expected everyone to help with daily and weekly chores. The girls all did their part, since Grace would not allow any slacking. Her favorite fable was, "The Little Red Hen." She would remind each of her daughters, "If you want to eat, you work."

Emma took the place of the son Matthew didn't have. She loved fishing and hunting with him. But she announced she planned to go off to college when she turned 18 to become a teacher. Matthew wanted a son to inherit the farm. So, a year later, Patricia was born. Everyone called her Patti.

Matthew's siblings shook their heads in disbelief when they found out that Matthew and Grace had another mouth to feed. While his brothers' wives did the required *oohing* and *ahhing* over the infant when Patti was baptized, they didn't offer cast-off dresses. It was their way of letting Grace know of their disapproval.

Despite Matthew's disappointment for the hoped-for son to inherit the Gunther & Sons farm after he passed, he loved all his daughters. He enjoyed spending time with each of them, especially Emma.

At the end of the day, Matthew and Emma would laugh as they read the comic strips together, especially the one featuring Blackie the cat. They'd laugh at the dance the cat did after jumping up high and landing on his two back feet to fight off an adversary.

The others spent time by themselves. Susan looked through the well-worn pages of her books and dreamed of traveling to faraway places. Paulina enjoyed making pretty things and spent hours embroidering dresses and scarves. Patti ran around the house and from family member to family member wanting to play. When she grew old enough, she learned to embroider and sew by making doll clothes from old scraps of material.

Grace played a game of solitaire if no one would play cards with her. Matthew and Emma also played the violins Grace's mother had given them as practice for playing on Sundays at their grandparents'. They had belonged to Grace's Papa Herman and Grandpa Samuel.

If there was any extra money after paying their share for the seed, Grace spent it on school activities for her daughters. She believed in her girls getting a good education so they could pursue life off the farm. Their clothes were made by resizing old dresses, coats, undergarments, and night garments for the girls, and shirts and pants for Matthew. They read week-old newspapers from Catherina. The girls waited for their turns after Matthew and Grace.

Many neighbors and the community believed Matthew and his family were living off George's and Catherina's benevolence.

They were unaware of the 50/50 financial arrangement to split profits *and* expenses. They were glad to see he was a hard worker but didn't understand why he failed to get his own farm with land prices so low.

Everyone did their work and the Gunther & Sons farm prospered. Everyone seemed happy with the arrangement for more than eleven years.

Grace – 1927 to 1939

Not everyone was happy. While Grace and Catherina were civil, Grace kept a wary eye on her mother-in-law. Catherina's constant criticisms were not welcomed. Life was hard and demanding enough without them. It was not how she had been raised. She vowed her daughters were not being raised that way either.

"The old woman's a battle-ax," Grace's third daughter, Paulina, would exclaim. "I can't do nothin' right enough."

Grace would correct her by saying, "The correct words are "cannot do anything right." You don't want to sound uneducated."

Paulina would toss her head and shrug her shoulders. "I don't care. I don't plan to live here any longer than I need to."

After Grace's daughters declared a silent mutiny, Matthew let Catherina know that his daughters were needed to help at home, especially with another mouth to feed.

Grace's greatest fear was that the promise of the farm wasn't in writing. She didn't trust her brothers-in-law and especially Maggie! They were shysters in her opinion—a word Paulina used often to describe them.

We were happier before we moved here, Grace often thought to herself while she kneaded the bread dough. *I'm appalled by Matthew's family's attitudes toward him, and how my daughters' cousins taunt them in school. It just isn't right.*

But Matthew brushed it off and maintained his optimistic outlook.

"Let it go in one ear and out the other," Matthew would tell his wife and girls. "Everything will work out." Matthew and Grace hadn't told them about their grandparents' promise.

"The reward," Matthew reminded Grace at night when they lay in bed whispering, "is someday this will be our home, our farm. We can live in the big house."

"What about all the talk about us being freeloaders, including the effect that has on your daughters?" Grace would ask. "Are you sure you want to continue living here?" She did hear about the gossip second-hand, usually, after Charlie's sons would ridicule her daughters, their cousins, to embarrass them.

Matthew responded in his normal patient tone of voice, "Have them hold their heads high. Pretend not to hear them. Someday all this sacrifice and hard work will be rewarded."

Grace heard what her husband said. But deep in her heart, she couldn't shake off a feeling of foreboding.

Charlie – June 11, 1939

It was a beautiful, sunny June day, with mid-day temperatures in the low 70s. Fluffy clouds moved slowly across the vivid blue sky, and the flowers and grasses waved in the light breeze. On the sort of day George loved most, he passed peacefully away in his sleep.

Although his pa had survived longer than anyone thought possible, Charlie felt a deep sadness. He would miss him and his sage advice. He hoped to be respected like him someday.

His fondest memories were of the times his pa, Matthew, and he spent fishing. Being the youngest two sons sometimes had its reward. George didn't have to work as hard since his older sons were able to do more of the work. But later, as the older brothers grew up and left home, the two younger brothers were left with all the chores.

Matthew had summoned Charlie on the day their pa passed.

It's because I live the closest. Charlie's three sons each mounted one of the workhorses to go tell the rest of the family. He hurried over to the old family farmhouse to see what he could do. When he arrived, Matthew left to get Grace.

Charlie found his ma seated in her old wooden rocker, rocking back and forth. She was reading the Bible out loud to herself with tears glistening in her eyes.

He took a seat next to her on the tall footstool Benjamin had built.

"I checked on him a couple hours after breakfast. He was gone," she said softly. "I knew immediately that he had departed to the House of the Lord. Then, I sat and prayed for his soul while holding his hand. He was a good man, and he built his legacy, one to be proud of."

As she spoke, he placed his weathered hands still smudged with dirt on her knee. She in turn placed her small, wrinkled hands atop his. They prayed together for George's soul until Matthew returned with Grace.

When his oldest brother, Jacob, arrived, Charlie could tell he felt slighted for not being the first one told as the oldest son. He knew that when Maggie arrived, she would feel the same way since she was the oldest child. There was a competition between the two of them over who would be in charge of the family when their pa passed. He hoped they would set aside their sibling rivalry to allow them to grieve in peace for their beloved pa.

After Maggie arrived and told everyone what they needed to do, Charlie took Catherina home with him for the evening.

The whole Gunther family attended the funeral at the local Methodist Church. Several of the crowd spilled out into the church's courtyard since there were not enough bench seats for everyone. Some sat in carriages or vehicles while the minister boomed out his sermon, which could be heard indoors and outside. Many people wept.

Everyone loved George and had stories to share. It was a testimony to his kindness. He always had a smile and a "howdy" whenever he passed someone on the road. He loved driving his Model T into town and walking around town. He'd stop and talk with everyone he met.

Before his strokes, everyone looked forward to seeing him on Saturdays. He'd visit all the business owners and walk around the town square with his grandson Nathaniel after checking on Maggie.

Charlie was thankful the storm clouds held off until after the burial and community potluck meal. Afterward, Matthew and his family hurried home because a sow was birthing piglets. They wanted to beat the storm.

Catherina stayed in town to greet everyone who had come to pay their respects. She planned to spend the night at Maggie's home. After Catherina bade goodnight to her children and their spouses, she closed the guest room door.

The storm outdoors had bypassed Harrison, but the inevitable feud that had been rumbling silently for years would be silent no longer.

Soon the brothers and Maggie began talking about their heritage: the Gunther & Sons farm. Rachel and Charlie initially stayed silent.

Charlie's brothers wanted to know how long they had to wait before doing what they wanted with the farm. Although no one had devised a clear plan, each brother had been selfishly thinking about it for years.

Charlie's dismay deepened after he suggested they wait until Matthew could join them and they refused. Sadly, they had only buried their father hours earlier.

He had looked at Rachel, his sister, and Melinda, his wife, with pain in his eyes. Each shrugged tearfully. They knew that Jacob and Maggie would challenge each other to be in charge.

It only got worse when Maggie declared that the farm was now theirs. Jacob and the rest of the brothers voiced their concerns about how to farm it.

Peter stated loudly, "Matthew and his family need to move out now. Ma and Pa aren't there to ensure he won't steal something from us."

"You never know what he'll do next. Mark my word, he's a thief," Peter continued.

Charlie shook his head and said, "He's been a great brother and a hard worker. He's done more than his share of the work." He glared at Peter. Rachel and Melinda both nodded, seconding what Charlie had said.

Benjamin agreed by saying, "He's lived there for twelve years. Everyone, including Ma and Pa, has spoken of his strong work ethic. They have been thankful he had been able to take over for Pa." Benjamin was careful not to look at Peter.

Peter rebutted, "Actually, he's been there for eleven and a half years—not twelve years. He came in November of 1927."

Benjamin rolled his eyes before replying, "And, how does that matter?"

Everyone jumped in with their opinions until Rachel dropped a book on the floor to get their attention.

Before Rachel could speak, her brothers gave all the women in the room a disapproving look that meant they were to be silent.

But Rachel and Maggie would not be silenced. After all, this was their inheritance too and they were not going to let their brothers forget it.

Rachel seconded Benjamin's statement supporting Matthew. She added forcefully, "He's easy to please, even when Ma wasn't. Even Ma praised Matthew for his efforts when I came home every July."

The siblings finally agreed half-heartedly to wait until after harvest before making any decisions. Their greatest fear was if they did something now, the work would fall on them. They had more than enough to do with their own farms during this time of the year and didn't need the added burden.

Then Melinda spoke up, "Where will Matthew's family live?"

Maggie stated with authority, "He's been freeloading off our parents for twelve years. They need to leave. But I suppose we should do the Christian thing and let them stay for now." She glared at Peter, daring him to correct her.

The stars were blinking off and on as the warm spring day evaporated during the ride home. Charlie and Melinda sat close to each other on the wagon bench. The horses knew their way home along the dirt road. Jacob and his family had already passed by in their auto, leaving their dust behind. They saw the eyes of a couple of deer and foxes on their three-mile journey.

Charlie spoke to Melinda in halting sentences, "I hope … they honor family … because it's important. Not because … the community or townspeople will think badly of us. We … need to treat each other … as family."

He could feel Melinda nodding her agreement on his shoulder. Even though the night had darkened, Charlie slapped the reins on the horses' backs to get them moving faster. He moved his arm to hug Melinda closer, seeking comfort from the pain of his pa's departure from this life.

But her warmth didn't stop the chill of premonition he felt. Something bad was going to happen. He just didn't know what it was or how he could prevent it.

PART 3

The black sheep in the family are often the ones who can foresee a future of family unity if other members are willing to let go of the past.

Rachel – 1916 to 1920

Rachel slept poorly throughout the month of May. Her anxiety over the decision she'd made caused her to hope for daylight to take away the fearful thoughts that erupted during the darkness.

She did her best to be still since Maggie lay next to her in the four-poster bed in the girls' bedroom. Although her sister was only three inches taller than she, Maggie seemed to be taking up far more than her half of the bed. While it was now her room, Maggie had been sleeping there next to her for the past two weeks. Nathaniel, her seven-year-old nephew, slept in a small bed in the same room.

Maggie's voice snarled in her ear, "Lie still. I have to get up early and go into town." She felt a kick on her shin.

Rachel hissed back, "Leaving me black and blue won't make me sleep better." She smiled to herself as she turned on her side. *I'm not afraid of Maggie's threats ... I can take care of myself.*

Her fears had started growing after the first weekend in May. She'd been awakened on Saturday night when her pa had left in the middle of the night with another horse rider. Later she learned it had been the sheriff. It was unusual for her pa to ride a horse since he loved driving his Model T. The next morning, she awoke before the sun crested the horizon and glimpsed him riding the horse back into the barn.

Uh-oh! Something happened. She'd hurriedly washed and dressed and gone down into the kitchen where her ma was finishing preparation for a big pre-church family breakfast. But no one said a word as they ate breakfast together. Everyone except Benjamin was there after their pa joined them. No one mentioned him.

As they were leaving for church, she spotted Benjamin trudging up the drive on foot with his head down. He didn't look good.

After they had attended church, Maggie and Nathaniel returned to the family farm in her pa's Model T with a suitcase. It took several days before Rachel learned that Nathan, Maggie's husband, had left in the middle of the night. No one said what had happened.

Finally, she confronted Benjamin after the mid-day family dinner.

"What happened?"

Benjamin refused to look at her and toed the dirt with his workboot.

"Are you okay? You don't look so good."

He'd shrugged and walked away with saying a word. Later she heard he'd fallen asleep in the hayloft until the next morning.

As she was doing her kitchen chores before walking to school, Rachel learned from her mother that Maggie was now in charge of the general store in Harrison, even though her husband, Nathan, and Nathan's father still owned it. Her pa drove Maggie and Nathaniel into town right after breakfast so Maggie could open the store. Then each night he went back to help her close it. This continued for several months.

Rachel was the one person in the family who could uncover secrets because she was unafraid to ask questions. But this time no one was saying anything. She was baffled about what could have happened that kept everyone so quiet.

She even asked Maggie what had happened at night as they waited to fall asleep. Maggie would say nothing.

She prayed whatever it was wouldn't ruin her own life plans.

In a week, Rachel would graduate from high school. She hoped whatever debacle Maggie had created wouldn't stop the ceremony or big family picnic. Or change her pa's mind about allowing her to travel to Madison with her best friend, Cora.

Rachel knew in her heart what she needed to do but wondering whether it was the right thing to do made her apprehensive. The fear of being disowned by her family haunted her. She was considered the "good" daughter, now, more than ever after whatever had happened with Maggie.

The church pastor preached about honoring one's parents. She loved her parents but couldn't abide by their expectations that she marry a farmer. Bear his children. Be a good Christian woman. Die.

Rachel knew that when she left home, she would not be returning … ever. She knew her parents, brothers, and sister would be angry at her. And the local farmers and church would say prayers for her wayward behavior! She'd be deemed the black sheep of the family. They believed that any good single girl of her age—soon-to-be 18—lived with her family until she married.

Her parents were insisting she marry the son of a farmer who lived in the next town over. Her pa had checked on the farmer by talking with Cora's father, the bank owner in Harrison. He'd found the farmer to have an honorable reputation, with some money in the bank. They believed the farmer's only son would inherit the farm and be a good provider and husband.

Rachel had other opinions about that, too, but no one was willing to listen to her. She had heard from her older brother, Benjamin, and others that the son had gambling and drinking problems. No way that marriage was going to happen!

Engaging in a debate wasn't part of her plans. She was well-liked by people because she didn't correct them or tell them what to think. Being in control was something Maggie relished. It was why she and her brothers and their families kept quiet and hoped Maggie didn't find out when they disagreed with her.

Also, Jacob and Peter were concerned when they heard Maggie was divorcing Nathan and taking over the general store. Women didn't get divorces. They didn't own stores. They were embarrassed their sister was being so brazen but confused because their pa was helping her and had given his approval and support. The gossip was a bit much to handle, especially since no one knew the truth about why it had happened.

So far, the plans for Rachel's escape were in motion. She wasn't going to allow Maggie's troubles to get in her way. If she had to, she'd leave during the night or go into town and hop a train out of here. But. She. Was. Not. Staying.

Cora and she were secretly earning and saving money. Cora's only brother Adam was studying to be a lawyer at the University of Wisconsin.

For weeks, she had been cajoling her pa to let her make the trip. He finally agreed after talking with Cora's father, who owned the local bank. She could go with Cora to visit Adam in Madison the week after high school graduation. Adam agreed to welcome the two girls and knew of their real plans. While Cora hoped her best friend would marry her brother, both Adam and Rachel knew it wouldn't happen. Adam had an adamant desire to remain a bachelor. No one knew why and it never occurred to Rachel to ask him, which was unusual, given her quizzical nature.

Adam was a good friend of Benjamin's and there were times he'd come out and help with harvest before he left Harrison to live in Madison. This further convinced Pa to agree to the visit.

"Two weeks is all. You're needed here," George said to her. "I want to find the best husband for my prettiest daughter."

Rachel had smiled, yet she had no intention of returning. She had no interest in being a hard-working farm wife. There were too many sacrifices her sisters-in-law made. Struggles her brothers endured. She didn't look down on them for choosing to live as farmers. It just wasn't what she wanted her own life to look like.

Maggie's story was different. She had snagged a general store owner in town. But, even in married life, Maggie sounded more and more like their critical mother. It was embarrassing for a woman to be so bossy. Now, Maggie's husband Nathan had left town with his father, and rumors as to why they weren't coming back circled and buzzed like nasty wasps.

Excited about their upcoming trip, Rachel and Cora ignored gossip and managed to keep their secret, secret. The "Maggie incident" helped since it diverted attention from them.

Five days after the graduation celebration it was finally time! They had packed more than necessary for their two-week stay. They had bought a few new dresses to wear once they arrived in Madison, Wisconsin. Each had stuffed small items in their undergarments and hoped they could close their trunks. Their families could send anything else later. Of course, first, they would need forgiveness for their deception.

They were careful to say all the right things to the few family members who had come to see them off at the train station. Most of Rachel's family were busy working in their fields this time of the year.

They smiled kindly at those reminding them how to transfer in Chicago. She and Cora didn't mention that Adam was meeting them there since he was on break from law school. The three planned on spending a few hours walking around the city before catching the last train to Madison. They didn't mention it out of fear their parents would reconsider. Since Chicago was the hub for all railroads, there was also a concern about anti-war protests going on in the city.

Over the next week, Cora and Rachel learned their way around the big town of Madison. They were pleased to hear that a factory was hiring men *and* women for factory jobs working on an assembly line. Even though the women were paid less than their male counterparts, Cora and Rachel felt happy to get the jobs.

Some American men were joining the WWI fight before the United States joined the Allies in April 1917. Rachel, being a farm girl, was young and strong and Cora, a town girl, did the best she could to keep up. While it was hard work, they loved the opportunity to be on their own and to make their own money.

Rachel sent a telegram back to her parents letting them know she was staying to do her patriotic duty. She hoped that would soothe the upset she was sure her pa and ma felt.

They telegrammed her back several times to be careful. In letters she received, they reminded her she was a small-town farm girl living alone in a large, dangerous town. They didn't want her reputation damaged for marriage.

While Adam had escorted Rachel and Cora around town for several weeks, soon they were able to get around without him. Yet they were careful to stay out of certain areas. Both had small pocket knives hidden in their dress pockets for protection.

After Rachel had been working on the line for a year, her boss learned she had a high school diploma (rare for a farm girl) and was good with numbers. The following week she was assigned to the bookkeeping department based on her boss's recommendation. The former clerk had left to return home and get married to her boyfriend who wanted to enlist in the war.

By then, Rachel had stopped sending the costly weekly telegrams about fulfilling her duty. Instead, she started sending letters twice a month letting the family know of her new job and that she was well.

In return, she received letters back from her ma with footnotes from her pa warning her to be careful with all the political unrest afoot. When she shared her letters with Cora, Rachel would shrug and say, "Well … I could go back … but to what?"

In early 1919, Cora was also promoted to the clerical pool but it only last two months. She had developed a romantic relationship with a soldier who had returned home and had stopped in Madison to see a comrade in his war unit. In May, they were married after Adam's graduation ceremony.

Cora and her husband left a week later to live in a small town in Iowa with his family living close by. Rachel's best friend kept encouraging her to come live there too. She had several candidates picked out for Rachel to marry.

But Rachel said no after visiting her friend once. The town was too reminiscent of the life she had left in Illinois.

Also, she felt betrayed by Cora marrying and leaving her behind in Madison. She missed their late-night chats about men and life, the adventures they had. Both girls enjoyed attending events in the small city and were careful. They had promised each other to be there for each other always, and now Cora had left her alone. But Rachel made new friends. She was staying.

Rachel loved living in Madison and the University of Wisconsin was growing. It was a great area for having intellectual conversations and experiencing new things. She loved the library, travel lectures, and other entertainment available on weekends. It was a far cry from the dull farm life she had once lived.

Often Adam met her after work, and he would introduce her to some of his friends. She would introduce him and his friends to the gals from the clerical and accounting pools who joined them. It was a fun and friendly time … some of the guys and gals got married. Others moved to Chicago for better work and marriage prospects. But Adam and Rachel stayed.

On July 1, 1919, when the company shut down for two weeks, Rachel decided it was time to finally travel back home to see her family. She was nervous and wasn't sure how she would be accepted. It was her first visit since arriving in Madison.

The plan was to stay with Maggie, since she was the only one with indoor plumbing. According to her ma's letters, Maggie's divorce had been finalized. She now owned the general store and a new Victorian home on one of the side streets lined with trees—a feat for a young woman, especially one with a son. The other Victorian home that Nathan's father had bought Nathan and Maggie as a wedding gift had been sold.

Maggie picked her up at the train station in her auto. After she had shown her sister the guest room, which had been nicely decorated, Maggie couldn't wait any longer. She started cajoling her into staying to fulfill her duty to her family.

"You need to do the right thing by marrying a farmer, or at least one of the single older men in town. The war is over. I can tell you who has the money," Maggie confided.

Rachel shrugged and sighed with exasperation. She knew her sister would never understand her need to leave. There were no regrets about leaving but did miss her family. But her family didn't understand her need to go and were not happy or supportive of her choice. Since they all believed she had stayed away to support the war effort, which had ended in 1918, it was now time to move back to Harrison and get married.

Maggie reminded her over the next ten days, "You need to do what Pa and Ma expect of you. Our parents aren't getting any younger. When you left, they were devastated. Living on your own as a working woman isn't the life your parents would choose for you. You're dishonoring them by living your life this way. You've become the black sheep in this family, which is embarrassing to all of us."

Maggie didn't see the irony in her comments. She owned a store and home and was divorced! Each was unusual for women, but all three? No one knew or shared with her why Maggie had divorced Nathan. While Maggie wasn't the first divorced woman in the community, she was in the family. Rachel knew her pa had been involved in making sure it all happened legally. What no one knew was why. Still, no one was talking, which was strange because the town thrived on gossip.

Because of the Gunther name, Maggie was able to be accepted over time as the sole owner of the general store in Harrison, even though it would take years for the community to broadly accept women working outside the home. Many didn't believe the sisters understood their true place in life.

Everyone had their say about their disappointment in Rachel. But no one stopped her from boarding the train ten days later for her trek back to her home in Madison.

Rachel – 1920 to 1939

As the years went by, Rachel created a tradition of visiting her family each July. Each year Maggie would pick her up at the train station and attempt to convince her to move back to where she belonged. Rachel continued ignoring her badgering and taunts.

After Pa had had several strokes, Maggie included guilt in her annual rants towards her wayward sister.

Maggie would say with reproach, "You know, ma has too much responsibility on her shoulders. With Pa's strokes, she needs your help. The rest of us are too busy earning a living to do more. You're so selfish living so far away."

The manipulations never worked. They only served to create more distrust and distance between the two sisters.

During her visits, Rachel heard about Maggie's reputation for being outspoken and bossy. While these were traits needed to run a store, manage employees, and be profitable, they weren't ladylike, nor welcomed during family interactions. It took many years before folks in the area stopped gossiping about it. Because of Maggie's fair prices and the quality of her merchandise, many became hard-won customers.

Rachel kept her own counsel and didn't participate in any gossip about Maggie.

Maggie was still her sister. She would defend her when people made rude or unkind comments about her. She didn't know if these comments were aimed at Maggie because she was a woman or if tarnishing the Gunther name added glee to their gossip. Their father's honorable reputation didn't stop the fault-finders, along with Peter, from gossiping.

Each year Rachel spent time with her sister and nephew Nathaniel, until he moved away from home to attend the University of Illinois. She would hitch a ride out to her parents' and each of her brothers' farms. She would visit them and friends who still lived in the community where she had grown up.

She would arrive with soft hands from her office work. Her sisters-in-law would compare their hands with hers. When she asked what she could do to help, they would sneer, "Nothing. Wouldn't want to ruin those soft hands."

Nevertheless, she always lent a hand by finding something productive to do. As she worked, she kept a smile on her face and sang a song, melting any animosity they felt towards her. Soon, one by one they would join in singing, then chattering with one another as in old times.

At the end of each visit, she left her hometown exhausted by all the small-town expectations and the growing discord in the Gunther family. It was difficult for her to put her finger on why it was happening ... but it bothered her that the threads of family unity were disintegrating.

During her travel home, she would say a grateful prayer of thanks that she no longer lived there. She would hop the train north back to her home in Madison, traveling through Chicago. She never told anyone she enjoyed spending a few hours walking and window-shopping in Chicago while waiting for the last train to Madison. It would have worried her parents all the more for her safety.

Over the years, when her nephews and nieces married, she sent a nice gift, ensuring the gift costs were the same for each. Yet she didn't attend the ceremonies and family gatherings. She stopped sending gifts when the next generation began marrying because there were so many of them, George and Catherina's great-grandchildren.

Despite her reasonable rationale, several felt hurt and believed Rachel thought she was too good to still be part of the family. Again, each year, she would soothe hurt feelings during her visit if they or their parents still lived in the area.

She hoped that with the passage of time, her parents and siblings would come to accept her lifestyle choice and to be supportive. Also, she hoped that they would stop gossiping and spreading half-truths about each other. It was appalling when her nieces and nephews began parroting their parents. The only difference was that their parents would wait until she left the room or returned home before voicing their opinions. Her nieces and nephews were less thoughtful.

She lamented that as women they were still second-class citizens. It wasn't until 1920 that women gained the right to vote. Although Rachel marched along with the suffragettes, because she valued her job, income, and independence too much, she never carried a sign during the marches. You never knew when someone had a camera, and your picture would be posted in the newspapers. Her greatest vow was to never need to return to live on her parents' farm. That was paramount in every decision she made.

When she had saved enough money, she purchased her own home. Several years later, she decided it was too much work. Homeownership limited her ability to travel, embroider, read, and attend events in Madison and Chicago. In the summer, the care of her beloved flower and vegetable gardens prevented her from spending time doing other things she enjoyed. Plus, she didn't have the green thumb her ma had. She worked from 8 a.m. to closing, usually around 6 p.m.

So she sold the house and bought a brand-new apartment close to work.

A banker friend of Adam's handled the transaction. She had netted a very nice return. But he made the mistake of commenting, "Women have no business owning property. See what happens? You had to sell it. When you buy property, it's for life."

She smiled and responded sweetly, "Really … hmm … well. How many men do you know would receive such a huge amount of cash on an investment? I'm not aware of any laws stating you are forever *burdened* by your property."

He didn't even have the politeness to look chagrined.

She shook her head at his graceless comment as he handed her the check and asked, "Do you want your money kept where it's safe? You know, women can never be too careful."

She smiled with polite grace and said, "Let me think about it." Instead, she deposited her money in another bank, after keeping part of it for her mattress.

Her pa had always cautioned her to have cash handy.

Over the next couple of years, Rachel received several promotions acceptable for women. Her petite 5' 3" stature caused male supervisors to discount her qualifications for any job other than bookkeeping or basic accounting. They didn't believe she would be strong enough to command enough authority to lead others.

But the owner of the company, Albert, was a visionary. He had allowed his foreman to hire women for the line before the country entered WWI. A year later, he'd switched the small manufacturing company from making parts needed to build aircraft during the war to making farm implements just as it ended.

He had different ideas about people and their qualifications. He'd noticed her taking notes in meetings using stenography and discovered she'd taken a class in high school, so he asked her to become his secretary in 1925. The way she handled herself in different situations was also impressive. The biggest plus was she didn't get upset when he was gruff and she could bring a smile to his face, just like she used to do with her pa and brothers.

Albert was a short, divorced man with a comb-over to hide his balding head. He had three grown children, who visited him when they needed money. Over the next several months, Albert and she became good friends, and she, his confidante.

She enjoyed conversations with him and his quick mind. But most importantly, he valued her advice, even though he didn't always take it. They started dating and married a year later in a private ceremony in 1926. She felt fortunate to find a man who considered her thoughts and ideas equal in many ways, although she was careful to behave according to society's expectations as a woman married to a wealthy man.

He wanted her to be his sole heir when he died. They talked it over with a lawyer friend of Adam's who worked in Chicago. In most cases, Albert's desires would have been easy to write up in a will. But due to the greed of his three children and ex-wife, she feared there would be a long, drawn-out fight if he died first. It was a fight she refused to be part of.

She had met each of his children after they were married and had listened to their lofty ideas about money. Yet each failed to save or work for it. They relied on their father to bail them out and pay for their desired lifestyles, playing upon Albert's guilt for leaving their mother. She also knew about his ex-wife's demands for more money after the divorce more than a decade ago.

Rachel had her own money that she kept in her maiden name, as her lawyer and Albert both advised. Otherwise, her money would become part of Albert's estate, if he died before she did. Given that he was fifteen years her senior, there was a good chance he would.

They stayed silent about the marriage with her family and Rachel rented out her apartment.

Each year, Rachel would travel alone to visit her family. She didn't need to add to their worries about her marrying a wealthy, divorced man with greedy children. The jewelry was left at home. But she once made the mistake of wearing her nicer clothes the first day of her visit after her marriage. After enduring comments that day about "coming up in the world," she had Maggie stay open late and bought a couple of house-dresses for her visits to the rest of her family's homes. In the future, she only packed her older clothes to take with her, and never wore the treasured string of pearls that Albert had bought her.

When the Great Depression began in 1927, it saddened her to have to camouflage her lifestyle, but she knew it would only upset the family dynamic if the second daughter in the family was wealthier than all of them. She'd seen how Maggie struggled and continued to struggle against the gossip. It was the reason Maggie didn't remarry. No man wanted a bossy woman who made more money than he. And no wealthy man in Harrison wanted to contend with an opinionated wife.

Rachel's surprise was that Maggie hadn't become more sympathetic towards others. In fact, she had become more righteous and pious than ever. It made the annual week home (she'd reduced it from ten days to seven) a challenge. Each year it became harder to listen to the staunch family beliefs and damaging gossip about each family member.

The year after their marriage, Albert sold his company. Before the sale, he bequeathed equal shares to her, each of his children, and his ex-wife, with Rachel's blessing. Rachel cashed out her shares and deposited the proceeds in her secret nest egg under her maiden name.

Rachel did share her happiness about her marriage with Matthew and his family. She knew they could keep a secret and be happy for her.

One Sunday afternoon, Rachel asked, "Albert, do you have a few minutes to talk?"

He'd been reading the newspaper and laid it down before patting the seat next to him on the divan. He made himself available whenever she needed to talk with him, just like she did with him.

She sat and gave him a sad smile, "I don't know what to do about my family's never-ending upset with each other. The way they talk about Matthew and his family, and about each other, I just don't understand it. It just doesn't end. All the fault-finding. In fact, seems to get worse each year. Many times, they don't know the truth, but make it up! I feel especially sorry for my nieces and sister-in-law to live that way."

Albert looked at her and said, "Yes, Matthew is a hard worker. He gets along well with his parents, and most of your siblings don't. There's jealousy. His daughters are also hard workers and are being well-educated. It scares them.

"There's nothing you can do. If your family wanted to get along, they'd make the effort. Just like my children would if they really wanted to do so. But, as you know, some people carry anger and upset in their hearts for their entire lives. They cling to the past and fail to create a better future. We can't change that."

Rachel nodded as he put his arm around her. She laid her head on his shoulder.

She appreciated Albert's sage advice. But it still hurt to think there was nothing she could do to change their ways. It was the illusion of family that bothered her the most. The way they talked about each other was considered acceptable. But it wasn't in her way of thinking. They needed to try to be kinder to one another.

When Albert died five years later from cancer in 1935, Matthew's daughter Emma sent a small floral arrangement from her parents and sisters. The rest of her family knew nothing about the marriage and never would.

As predicted, Albert's three children, who rarely visited their father and never did anything to help him during his illness, demanded their money. Under estate law, she was entitled to the home and half of the monies. Knowing that the vultures would swoop in to take all the household goods they considered valuable, Rachel had removed those items she wanted to keep during Albert's illness, with his blessing.

She settled out of court just to get it over with; otherwise, she'd spend time and money fighting them to keep what was hers. One of Albert's sons had gambling debts and his daughter's home was being foreclosed on. They'd already cashed in their stock options. Even though she knew it was coming, it was still nasty as they had discussed when Albert was alive. No one won, except the attorneys.

But Rachel had saved wisely and moved back into her apartment a wealthy woman who volunteered her time to help other women. She didn't need to work after Albert's death.

Deceiving her family about her situation saddened her. But she got up every morning to work with charities that helped women, many with children, live and prosper on their own. She gave many of her old clothes away but kept several garments for her visits home. The Great Depression was a difficult time for everyone, especially women, since factories now only hired men for the few jobs available.

When Matthew's eldest daughter, Susan, turned 18 and graduated from high school, Rachel invited her to share her two-bedroom 1,000-square foot apartment in Madison. Susan got a job at the local drug store as a cashier since she had no interest in getting a college degree. They ate dinner together each night and enjoyed the university's lectures on travel and books. It was an enjoyable time, and they even took a couple of trips together. Then, in 1939, it was Emma's turn.

It became a rite of passage for Matthew's daughters to live with her away from the family strife and wagging tongues, especially after her pa passed.

Rachel – 1939

Rachel was devastated by her pa's death and marveled at how long he had survived. Susan and she traveled to Harrison to attend the funeral.

But only hours after her pa had been buried, she was horrified by her siblings' greed and comments about Matthew. She knew there was nothing she could do to change the tide of anger stoked by Peter and Maggie.

Thankfully, they had agreed to wait until after harvest before making any decisions about the Gunther & Sons farm. Her hope was that time would give her siblings the opportunity to see reason about how they planned to divide up the family farm. She stayed quiet about the growing feud while Susan and she traveled back to Madison the day after the funeral.

Rachel had heard gossip about Matthew freeloading during her visits back home. She didn't believe it and knew he was a hard worker, even though she didn't know about the agreement between him and their parents. She was angry at the lies but kept her silence and prayed the truth would eventually be told. Telling the truth now while everyone was grieving over pa's death would only fall on deaf ears and make things worse.

Farmers were stuck in time and stories. It helped them cope with things they could not control: weather, accidents, illnesses, and the economy. Some of her cousins were now working in factory jobs in Chicago or Detroit. They had no interest in farming and had a greater desire to receive a steady paycheck. But regardless of their life choices, she wished them the best.

Her parents had never visited her in Madison due to their farm responsibilities. Her brother, Benjamin, visited once before her marriage to Albert and stayed with his friend Adam. The next time he visited in 1938, she told him her plan about Susan and her sisters coming to live with her. He seemed happy for her and for them.

But a couple of weeks later, she received a missive from Maggie.

"If you want to be part of this family, you need to do what we tell you. You don't want to encourage Matthew's daughters to freeload like he's been doing all these years. His daughters need to learn their place in life by getting married. It's their only hope for a decent life and to be accepted in the family."

PART 4

Forgiveness is seeing life through the hearts of our souls, not through our judgments about the way we believe others should live their lives.

Maggie – June 1939

Maggie agonized all night after her siblings left her home following Pa's funeral. Now that he was buried, she decided it was up to her to take charge of the Gunther family affairs and not wait.

As the early morning birds started chirping, she got up and hurriedly dressed.

I'm not going to wait for them to muck this up. I need to keep my dignity in this town and honor my pa's good name, she thought to herself. But her mind churned with all the things that would need to be done, starting with removing Matthew and his family from the Gunther & Sons farm before something bad happened.

The first thing Maggie did was make sure the early loadings for customers were done right.

The next thing she did was put Clyde in charge of the store so she could go to Adam's office, a half-mile away. She had asked one of the church women after the funeral to take Catherina back to her farmhouse and stay with her for the day. She didn't want her ma to be alone and feared any solicitors that might show up since everyone in the area knew George had passed away. A widow could never be too careful, especially with the last name of Gunther.

Adam, Benjamin's and Rachel's friend, had moved his law practice back to Harrison when his father died and he inherited the bank. In turn, Adam hired a bank manager so he could focus on practicing law but remained chairman of the board.

Cora, Adam's sister, was now a widow. She had moved back to her hometown too along with one of her three children after her husband died. The three of them lived together in a big Victorian house. Adam had also set up a trust for Cora and her children, according to gossip.

Maggie was afraid of what would happen if her ma passed before this year's harvest or if one of her brothers created a big problem over the farm by saying the wrong thing.

It was in everyone's best interest that she obtain the will and be the sole executor. They lived in a community where most people liked her pa, and she didn't want his good name tarnished by a family feud. Maggie also didn't want Catherina to get in the way of the decisions she believed she needed to make on behalf of the family.

In her mind, it was her sole responsibility to tell her ma what was best, including where Catherina should live, how to divide up the farm, and who would inherit certain things like jewelry, furniture, etc. Since Nathaniel and her brothers' kids had all left home, except for those of Charlie and Matthew, who each had two kids living at home, they needed a place for their ma to live. It would need to be with one of her brothers. She would make sure Catherina was not moving into town to live with her. She was not going to be burdened with caretaking after she had worked so hard. It had taken decades, but now she was finally respected as a store owner and a town citizen despite being a woman.

Maggie

Maggie walked fast down the dusty street. She nodded at each person she encountered along the way with a smile but didn't encourage anyone to stop and talk with her. She was on a mission, and nothing was going to get in her way.

When she arrived at the law office, she paused and breathed before opening the glass door. She waited for her eyes to adjust to the dark office after walking in the bright sunshine. It took a moment to see Adam sitting behind his desk, reading under his green-glassed banker's lamp.

"Good morning," she said, businesslike.

Adam looked up from behind his desk and warmly replied, "Good morning to you, too."

"I'm sorry to hear about George's passing," Adam said. He had liked the old man. In fact, everyone in town liked him. He and his sister had attended the funeral. It was what people did in their community.

"I need to see what we can do about the Gunther farm." Maggie looked directly at Adam, with a hesitant edge in her voice. "As you know, my ma is now living there by herself. We need to find her a place to live. We haven't found a will."

Adam stood and gestured for her to take a seat on the opposite side of the desk. Then, he closed the file he had been working on before the interruption.

"What makes you think there isn't a will?" Adam asked as he leaned back in his padded swivel chair. He took care to soften his tone of voice. Maggie's reputation preceded her, and he didn't need her to upset his day or leave upset with him.

"I didn't find one. My ma wouldn't say anything about it one way or the other when I questioned her before the funeral ... the day before yesterday," Maggie stated. "So, I assume there isn't one."

Adam rocked back and forth in his chair as he thought out loud. "Well, let me look in my records to see if I've done any work for your parents."

"Why do you need to do that?" Maggie asked, frowning. "Time is important since my ma could pass away soon, or someone could take advantage of her."

"If I've done previous work for your parents, it would be a conflict of interest for me to talk to you." Adam paused before clarifying, "About the farm, your mother, or your father's will." He looked down on his desk to find a notepad and pen.

"Huh?" Maggie sounded perplexed and sat back in her seat. "What difference would that make? I'm their eldest child so I have a right to know what is happening."

Adam resumed rocking in his chair after he'd written a note to himself.

"My pa only used quit claim deeds whenever he purchased other farmers' properties. I cannot imagine you've done any work for him. Have you? Did you write him a will? What other work would there be?" Maggie asked with nervous apprehension. She started twisting her clasped hands in her lap. *Why is he making this so hard?*

"Here's my recommendation." He paused to make sure he had her attention. "Let me look through my files to be sure I've not done any work for your parents. Meanwhile, you should walk over to the county office. Ask to see the property deed for the Gunther farm." Adam nodded towards the building across the street.

"Why?" Maggie asked. "My pa owned his farm free and clear."

"I can't comment further until I check my files. Give me a couple of days. I have some other work that requires my attention."

"Well, let me think about it," Maggie said. It upset her that she had to do more work than was necessary to take charge of her ma and the farm. But there wasn't another attorney in town whom she would trust with this very important issue and not create additional gossip.

Maggie

Two days later, Maggie reappeared in Adam's office, again without an appointment. "Well?" she asked after they acknowledged one another.

Adam said in a calm and polite tone, "Hello and good morning. I'll be with you as soon as I am finished, Maggie. I'm in the middle of reading something here."

Maggie stood waiting, tapping her foot. Then she stopped. *I need to remember patience.* She needed Adam on her side.

To calm herself, she turned to look outside. She watched as clouds darkened the sky above the county office across the street. *I hope that doesn't mean more rain. The farmers don't need another downpour like yesterday. It'll ruin their crops.* She sighed as she waited.

"What can I do for you?" Adam finally asked as he stood and gestured for Maggie to take a seat. He wanted them looking at each other and not have her towering over him.

"Well ... did you check your files?" Maggie asked.

"Yes. It appears that I haven't done any work for your parents in the past," Adam said.

Maggie let out a sigh of relief. "Well ... we need to get busy and issue whatever legal papers we need. I want to get my ma moved out of the farmhouse ..." Then, she added, "... for her own safety. A seventy-three-year-old woman shouldn't live alone. Especially when she has family living nearby that can take care of her."

Maggie paused to make sure Adam was listening to her. "Then, the farm needs to be divided up for each of my pa's children. My brothers and I need to have Matthew and his family move out. He needs to stop freeloading and get his own place," Maggie stopped and smiled tentatively. She wasn't feeling comfortable with the way he was watching her.

"Why?" Adam asked. He maintained his normal calm tone and didn't look away. He'd heard she could be difficult to work with when she didn't get her own way. But he was a friend of the family and was not going to be caught in the middle of a family fight. His sister and he had handled their own parents' estate amicably. At times it baffled him how easily family dissension could occur when people didn't get what they believed was rightfully theirs.

"Because it's the right thing to do," Maggie stated matter-of-factly. She was impatient to get things done. For some reason, she felt nervous about this discussion. *Why didn't he agree to do what I want done? He's the attorney and I'm the client.*

Adam paused before asking, "Did you check with the county office?" He nodded towards the building across the street.

"No. I didn't see a need to do so. The deed for the farm is in my pa's name. I don't know why I need to prove something that is obvious," Maggie stated with a bit of defiance. She sat back in her chair and rearranged her skirt to make sure her knees were covered.

"Well … let's get something very clear. If I'm going to help you and your family—your entire family—I'm working for the betterment of everyone. Not you alone. Or one of your brothers. Or someone else," Adam stated. He could see Maggie was frowning, unhappy about his declaration.

Before she could counter his remarks, he went on. "I've been a friend of the family for many decades, as were my parents. I do not want to get in the middle of a feud."

"There won't be one ... there cannot be one ... why would there be one?" Maggie asked, dumbfounded he would say such a thing.

All my siblings get along. Well, usually. Well, most of the time. Well ... there were a few times ...

"Well ... I talk with many folks from around here. I've seen your mother in town several times a month. She comes to visit the ladies from her church. These folks are no different from big city folks when it comes to wanting what they believe is theirs," Adam said. "When someone dies, family relationships can become strained, if not broken apart forever. We have this illusion of family that everyone gets along, even during the bad times. Sometimes they do. But there are many times when the branches of the family tree are severed ... forever. Even when no one thinks it could happen to their family."

He continued looking at her with a steady gaze.

Maggie blushed and felt confused by the entire conversation.

My ma never left the farm since Pa became an invalid. He must be mistaken. If she was in town, she never stopped by to see me. She always seemed too busy to come into the store to get what she needed and expected me to deliver it to her.

Maggie sighed and hoped Adam didn't notice. *The family usually got along ... and even after Peter's issue with Matthew ... we still view each other as family. I don't understand his point.*

Why is it so hard for him to do what I need to have done? He seems to be making this more difficult than my divorce attorney did. Of course, Pa had been involved and used his good name to be sure Nathaniel and I were protected.

As if reading her mind, he continued, "I didn't know if you would follow through and walk across the street. So, I went over. Public records are available for anyone to look at."

Maggie was losing patience. "So, what? Did you see that my pa owned the farm? The farm he's farmed for fifty-three years? What did that tell you?"

"What it told me is that Catherina owns it," Adam stated. "Just her. Only her," he added for emphasis.

It took Maggie a full minute before reality settled in.

The dynamite was launched.

"What? That's impossible. Why would a man list his wife as the sole owner?" Maggie screeched. "That's impossible!"

I had to fight my ex-husband and the county to have my name solely listed on the deed for the general store and the Victorian home we lived in when we divorced. But without Nathan's signature and agreement, regardless of the divorce decree, I couldn't be solely listed on the deed because I'm a woman. Thankfully Pa stepped in to make sure I got what was mine.

"Well … he listed her name on the deed … only her name," Adam replied. He watched her as several emotions danced across her face.

"There's no law against it," Adam added. He rocked back in his chair.

"She's now one of the richest women in the county … at least on paper," Adam shared with a grin on his face. He loved it when women were finally given their rights as people. He tapped his fingertips together.

He knew Maggie hated anyone besting her, including her mother or brothers, so he waited her out and watched as she wrestled with her emotions over this news.

"Impossible!" Maggie finally repeated. "There must be some mistake."

Adam stopped grinning.

"Well … I recommend you walk right on over there. Across the street. Check it out. It's a fact." Adam pointed at the courthouse.

"It really isn't that hard to do," he added with a slight smile to lighten the conversation.

Maggie was quiet for a minute, then asked, "Then what do we do? Isn't there a will?"

Adam asked, "A will for what? Your mother owns it now. All by herself."

"There's nothing we can do, as my pa's children? The ones that should rightfully own it now?" Maggie asked as she breathed to calm herself down and stay in control of the conversation. She refused to believe there was nothing she could do to change this bad turn of events.

"Well, there is a talk in Peoria tomorrow afternoon explaining wills and tax laws. There have been a lot of changes, especially with family farms. I'm planning on attending.

You're welcome to ride down to Peoria with me," Adam offered.

"What will that do?" Maggie asked skeptically. She had a store to run, and a ma and brother to evict from her pa's farm before they ruined the place. She didn't have time for all this nonsense.

"Well, if you can't find a will …" He paused. "There wasn't one filed at the county office, by the way—which means, you could help your mother make a will," Adam stated helpfully.

"That would be the right thing to do." Then, he quickly added, "… with her permission of course."

Maggie hesitated. She hated taking a day away from her store … it was why she never missed a day and never took a vacation. She had two clerks, but believed she had to be there to make sure everything was done the right way. But she wasn't going to disappoint her pa after he helped her get the store in her name and quell the gossip that could have ruined her and her son's future. It felt like yesterday instead of twenty-three years ago.

"I'm sure Clyde can handle the store for one day," Adam said, smiling.

"Or Lucille. Actually, she does a better job," Maggie retorted. *The way men think of women! Stop! Don't let him upset you. He's the one that can help you!*

"Whatever you believe is right," Adam graciously replied. He added a smile and shrugged before standing up. It was his polite way of signaling the end of their meeting.

A week later after they had attended the meeting on wills and tax laws, Adam provided her with a written *Last Will &*

Testament of Catherina Gunther for Catherina's signature. He cautioned her that if she didn't want to sign it, Maggie could not force her to do so.

He also cautioned Maggie in as strong a tone as he could muster and still be tactful, "If I hear of any intimidation or coercion from you or any family member, I will contact the town or county sheriff, depending on which church member told on you or your brothers. The farm is now solely owned by your mother."

Maggie frowned. She was taken aback by his statement. Then, she smiled and hugged the will to her like it was the most precious document she'd ever held.

"Don't forget to have the signature witnessed," Adam said in a slightly louder voice as Maggie turned away to hurry out the door.

As he watched her walk fast past his office windows, he knew Catherina could be obstinate when things weren't her idea.

Like mother, like daughter. Adam thought, crossing his fingers that this would go better than he feared.

Maggie – June 29, 1939

The next day, late in the afternoon after the account records and inventory had been finalized for the day, Maggie left Lucille in charge of the store. She drove the will out to the Gunther farm for her ma to sign. It was the second to last day of June and the summer afternoon was cooling down. She loved driving with the windows down and placed the will under a shawl to make sure the papers didn't fly out of the vehicle as she drove.

During the drive, she thought about all the government regulations she'd learned about. *Whew, that meeting only left me confused. It's too complicated,* she thought. *Good thing Adam knows what he's doing.*

As she drove, she paid careful attention to avoid any potholes still filled with water from the early afternoon rain. She marveled that many in their community had lost their family farms during the Great Depression. It was one of the most difficult economic periods in United States history. Those who were able to keep their property prospered and bought up other parcels during forced sales.

Her parents had prospered due to the help of their children, although there had been some rough times. She gave no special acknowledgment to the sacrifices of Matthew and his family. It never occurred to her to thank him or his family. After all, they had been freeloading for over a decade with no evidence of leaving. It was confusing to her and her brothers that Matthew didn't buy a farm from a distressed farmer.

Well, that will soon change. She didn't trust Matthew to do the right thing. He was very selfish to freeload all these years. Her biggest fear was her ma would give Matthew the farm or other things out of some sort of family obligation, and not think about her other children.

I'm the smart one, the one who got the best grades in school. The only one who got off the farm. Well, Rachel did, too. But she's some bookkeeper. Single, too. She doesn't count. My status as divorced is only a slight step up from the single women living in town. Being the eldest and smartest meant she had to stay ahead of the rest of them. It justified her belief that it was her obligation to speak up and make sure everything was done in the right way.

Well, now we will have this handled so that each of us seven kids knows what we have, and what to expect when Ma dies.

Upon her arrival, she found her ma seated on a straight-backed chair out under the willow tree. She was shelling the last of the peas picked from her garden.

Maggie greeted her.

Catherina looked up at her daughter, shading her eyes from the sun, with a pea pod still in her hand. She murmured, "Hello. What brings you out here this time of the day?"

Maggie jumped right in, "I've talked with Adam—you remember him, right?"

"Yes. He's Cora's brother. His pa was a friend and our banker before he died. I used to visit with his ma when she was alive," Catherina replied.

"Well ..." *Stay on track,* Maggie reminded herself. "With pa's death, we need to decide what to do about the farm."

Remember, Adam said to keep it general.

"Whatever for? What does he have to do with anything?" Catherina asked and threw the peapod into the bushel basket sitting at her feet. The hogs would love them for their dinner that evening.

"Adam is a lawyer. With pa … well … we need to decide as a family what to do next. You're getting older. We want to be sure we're not hurt financially when you pass …" Maggie stated, choosing her words with care, "… and you're taken care of."

"Whatever does all that mean?" Catherina asked. She shook her head and focused on shelling the final peas and tossing the greens pods. She stopped and sat still, knowing that when Magdalena stammered, she wasn't comfortable with what she was trying to say. It meant the listener needed to pay closer attention or suffer the consequences.

"I attended a meeting about wills last week," Maggie said with care. "Along with Adam," she added for credibility.

"So … what does that have to do with me?" Catherina asked. The sun was starting to drop behind the cornfield. The cooler evening breeze was gently whispering through the leaves. But it was too early for the fireflies to start blinking their hellos.

"Well … I had Adam draw up a will for you," Maggie said. With shaky hands, she thrust the papers out in front of her. When her ma failed to take them from her, she leaned down and thrust them into her hands.

Catherina said, looking down, "Let me read it later. It's too hot now." She felt nervous as she watched the papers flutter in the slight breeze.

Maggie doubted her ma would be able to read and understand the will. But she had to drive back into town before it became too dark. Again, she heard Adam's words echoing in her head not to intimidate or force her ma to sign.

She sighed. "Okay," she said. Then, she turned and left, thinking, *Next time, I'll need to leave Lucille in charge again and drive out earlier. This is going to take more time than I realized. I just hope Ma isn't dying anytime soon.*

Maggie – July 3, 1939

Three days passed. When the grandfather clock in the farmhouse chimed half-past five, Maggie returned. She parked her car by the barn and breathed in the smells of animal manure before opening the front door to the old house and calling out a greeting.

Catherina was seated at the kitchen table eating a dinner of homemade soup and bread.

After repeating her hello, she asked her mother, "Did you get a chance to read it?"

"Read what?" Catherina asked as she took her bread to sop up the last of the soup in her bowl.

Maggie replied, "The will."

"What will? Why is there a need for a will?" asked Catherina. She chewed on the small piece of homemade bread, which she had baked that day and slathered with homemade butter.

Maggie continued standing, talking with her hands as she explained the importance of a will. When she stopped talking and looked down at Catherina still seated in her chair, her ma threw up her hands and exclaimed, "Everything I have will go to all of you."

Maggie felt exasperated and said, in as patient a tone as she could muster, "I know, Ma. I just want to make sure it is legal. That all of us are protected."

"Trust in God," her ma proclaimed, again raising her arms.

Maggie cried, "Yes, and human nature being what it is, we need to get this signed now."

Catherina said, with frustration, "Well, I don't know where it is. Human nature hasn't changed in hundreds of years. So why now?"

Just then Matthew walked into the kitchen to let his ma know about the progress with the corn crop. He had left the workhorses resting in the lane adjacent to the field and the house. They were patiently waiting to be driven to the barn for their nighttime water and feed, along with a quick curry. Knee-high by the Fourth of July, which was tomorrow, was the sign of a good corn crop. Theirs was good.

"What's this all about?" Matthew said as he leaned down to pour a glass of water from the glass pitcher sitting on the kitchen table. He could tell Maggie and Catherina were unhappy with one another. Nothing unusual. He was curious what it was about this time.

Maggie said with care, "Her will."

Matthew's heart stopped for a moment. His face froze. His voice eked out the words, "What will?"

Maggie explained, "The one she needs to sign so we call get equal shares of the farm and minimize inheritance taxes." She smiled, happy she to be in charge.

Matthew shook his head in disbelief. His farm ... what? He sputtered, "What farm?"

Maggie exclaimed, her tone flint-hard, "Are you stupid? Been out in the sun too long? This farm!" She glared at him.

Becoming more nervous, Matthew exclaimed, "What do you mean, this ... farm?"

Maggie began to lose her temper. "This farm! Pa's farm. The Gunther & Sons farm. All of us get equal shares of this farm when ma dies."

Matthew stood there in shock and glanced down at his ma, who refused to look at him. Then, with an uncharacteristic hard edge in his voice, he looked directly at Maggie and exclaimed, "No. No, you don't! Not after working it for the past twelve years. No. You. Don't!"

Matthew rubbed his weathered hands, covered with dirt from the field, over his face, trying to clear his head. There was silence except for the grandfather clock chiming six times.

Then, he said deliberately, "Pa and Ma gave us—me and my family—this property. It's for all the years we've been living here, sweating here, and sacrificing to allow them to continue living here. It was our agreement. Pa's and Ma's promise to me. Pa and I shook hands."

Maggie was shocked, but quickly recovered and retorted, "No. They did not. They loved all of us. Not just you!"

They both looked down at their ma.

Catherina sat there with her shoulders hunched, staring at her wrinkled hands folded in her lap. She was fearful to utter a word.

Maggie had an uneasy feeling. She commanded in a loud tone, "Ma! Look at me. What did you do?"

Catherina said softly, refusing to look at either of them, "Nothing. I didn't do anything wrong."

Maggie was flabbergasted. She looked at Matthew and said in her most patronizing tone of voice, "Well, it's great you've been helping out and living here for free all these years. But there comes a time when you need to stand on your own two feet and farm your own place. Now. Is. That. Time." She pointed at him.

Maggie's mind raced. *Wait until I tell Jacob and my brothers about this. Who does Matthew think he is, anyway? Thinking this farm is his because he lived here for twelve years and worked it? He's really become a greedy cuss, hasn't he?*

Before she could continue, Matthew yelled in a shaky voice, "Helping out? You mean so the rest of you could move on, buy property, and make lots of money? You mean so Ma and Pa could keep this place?" He rarely spoke in a loud tone of voice, so it startled both women.

Matthew watched as his ma cringed from the yelling and grew smaller in her kitchen chair.

But that didn't stop him. He was a patient man. He had been dreaming of the day when the 500 acres would be all his—an acknowledgment to him and his family for all their hard work and sacrifice. A moment when he would prosper, too. His family and he could go into town with their heads held high ... feel respected. Just as had been promised to him on that cold winter evening in 1927. *Pa and I shook hands! A gentleman's agreement!*

Throughout the years, Grace and he had discussed how they would best handle it. They had discussed sharing some of the acreage with each of his brothers—plans that were in his head, not written down.

"See what you've done?" She gestured at their ma still hunched over in her chair, her face flushed. "I'm not sure what you're trying to cause here. This is unacceptable. You should be ashamed of yourself for trying to steal the family farm. It's rightfully everyone's!"

Then, as Matthew nervously shifted from one foot to the other, Maggie glared at both Catherina and him. Clenching and unclenching her hands, she looked like a cat waiting to pounce on its prey.

She struggled to calm herself but couldn't resist continuing. "How dare you try to steal your parents' farm. They worked so hard to keep it during all these years! They gave you and your family a home so you didn't have to work for Smythe. You should be ashamed. You should go and get your own farm. You've been living off Ma and Pa far too long!"

After glaring at each of them, she turned on her heel and stormed out of the house, slamming the front door behind her. She drove back into town seething at Matthew's greed and blaming him for tearing the family apart.

After the swirl of hatred and anger left, Matthew stood there in a daze, shaking. He stared down at his ma with tears rolling down his sweaty face. She remained seated at the table with downcast, weeping eyes. Catherina's tears were a rarity. She sat with her hands clasped and her lips moving, as if in prayer.

He shook his head at the sight, devoid of any feelings for the woman. She'd ripped out his heart and soul. It didn't occur to him she was crying because of the travesty that had just occurred and the depth of heartbreak of losing her husband and now her family.

He left the kitchen and walked toward his horses in a daze.

He murmured out loud to himself, "My own ma. How dare she give away what is mine. After all that work! All the sacrifice and struggle my family and I have endured! It's my farm. I kept it alive and growing for them! We made so many sacrifices to keep Pa's dream of being a well-respected and prosperous farmer alive. This. Isn't. Right. It's. Not. Fair."

His shock was turning into anger. He could feel it erupting from within. He didn't know what to do or how to express these feelings since he didn't experience them often. This was unimaginable. His mind struggled to register what had happened. It felt like his life was over.

It never occurred to him to be angry with his pa, even though George had had twelve years to put his promise in writing. Matthew was angry at his ma for not honoring his pa's promise. She had been there. She had agreed. It was her responsibility to tell the truth now.

Catherina never forgot that fateful day back in 1939 or Matthew staring at her with the saddest eyes she had ever seen. It had shocked her to the core to experience that depth of sorrow and feelings of betrayal.

Matthew never cried and seldom showed any emotion for most of his life. After he left, she ran to the window and watched her son in quiet sadness as he swayed as if in a daze walking toward the team of horses. She continued watching as he gathered the reins and snapped them in the air while saying, "Gee." The horses moved on slowly as Catherina stood in the window watching until the fireflies began lighting up the evening.

It was at that moment when George's desires to leave a benevolent family legacy of unity and prosperity were disavowed, repeating the same fate he had endured when his own pa had died.

Matthew

Dusk was softly turning darker as Matthew drove his team to the barn. Soon, the only light was from the fireflies flickering along the farm lane. His world had turned from a bright expectation of another corn harvest to a depth of sadness he'd never experienced before. He didn't know what to do or how to handle it.

He barely noticed the flickering of the fireflies. *When fireflies light your path home ...* He didn't know where those words came from. He followed the horses, numb, allowing them to lead the way.

He was too afraid to think. Unable to feel anything. Or, to put any feelings into words.

Without thought, he went through the motions of feeding the horses. He brushed them down as fast as he could, then cleaned out their stalls. It was all done with no thought about what he was doing.

It wasn't until Emma came to tell him dinner was ready that he left the comfort of the horses and the musty smells of the barn. Together, they walked the half-mile home, not speaking. His devastation was written on his face and in his walk. His life was over. His whole world as a farmer had been stripped away from him. He couldn't even shed a tear.

Emma walked beside her father without saying a word. She was sad to see that something bad had happened but didn't know what it was or what to say. She couldn't know this fateful family legacy would impact her own family someday.

Late that night Matthew suddenly awoke and sat up in bed. "Oh!" Glancing over at Grace and seeing she was still asleep, he breathed.

Then he remembered the dream that woke him.

"The will wasn't signed. Pa told me that the deed was in ma's name. Ma still owns the farm. All of it." He then lay back down and slept with more optimism.

PART 5

We all forget the beautiful memories during our life and focus on our regrets, the way situations should have happened, and the words that should have been said.

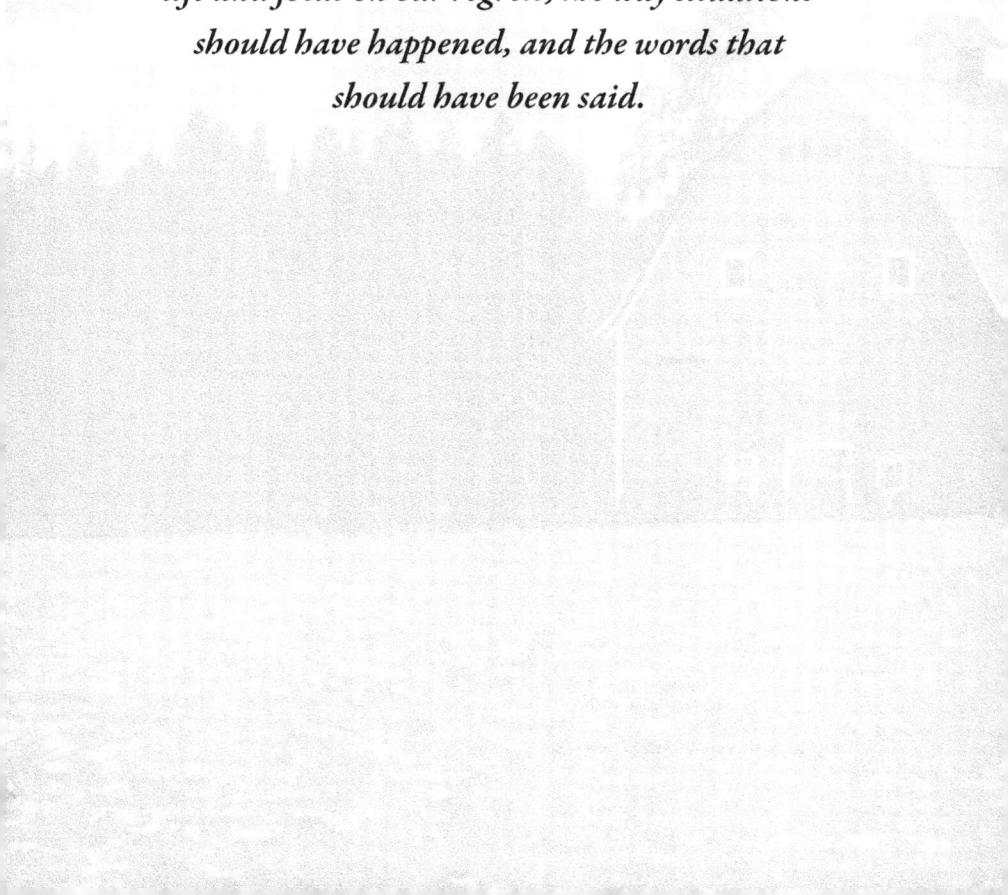

Benjamin – 1916 to 1939

Benjamin was 22 when he returned home after training to fight in WWI but had never left the United States soil to fight. Instead, he had been assigned a desk job because of his good math skills.

But the memories of feeling like he'd messed up before he left came rushing back as soon as he stepped off the train back in Harrison.

After several days of working on the farm, he decided to become the type of man his pa and ma expected him to become. He would never again look his pa in the eye and see the depth of hurt and disappointment he'd caused following that night of the "Maggie incident."

His siblings, the townspeople, and neighboring farmers never knew anything about what happened that night, which left many to speculate about why his brother-in-law and Nathan's father had left town so suddenly. He wasn't talking after his pa warned him not to do so. It had felt like a threat of being severed from the Gunther family.

"It would hurt Maggie and Nathaniel, and their ability to live here in Harrison," George had told Benjamin. He never wanted to be the cause of gossip or bad will, especially towards his family.

He doubted his ma knew the truth either. Pa and he had acted very quickly to curb any news about the ordeal with the help of the sheriff. After that night, he drank only one beer at a time, even during the Prohibition years, and stopped playing poker for money while living in the Harrison area. But he had indulged both passions, along with his comrades, when being trained for the war effort.

"I'm sorry you were involved in all that happened with Nathan and that woman. It doesn't excuse you for drinking too much and being involved in that mess. Let this be a lesson to never allow alcohol, poker, women, and money to mix again. If you can't do this, you need to move far away. I won't have you trash the Gunther name after all the hard work your ma and I have done to live here for so many years," George had said with anger in his voice.

After Benjamin had spent the night in jail, all charges were dropped, since all he'd done was join in a poker game. But his pa had told him, "You need to walk home and think about the life you really want to have. I won't bail you out again." George had mounted his horse for the ride back to the farm.

While George never whipped his kids or used his belt, Benjamin still felt like he'd been whipped with the shame of what had happened, even though he felt it was unwarranted that day.

Benjamin never understood how Maggie knew that he knew the truth. She had never asked him about it and it caused an uneasy truce between them. She knew enough to win the divorce and sole ownership of the general store due to their pa's intervention with the lawyer he hired. They were still pleasant to one another when they saw each other in town, or when he stopped by the general store. He didn't care what she did as long as she didn't blame him for what had happened to Nathan. Sadly, everyone overlooked Nathaniel's feelings about it and was often surprised by his anger at his father's leaving.

He never understood why it was called the "Maggie incident" in his family. She hadn't been involved. But the aftermath impacted her and his nephew in a cruel way due to the divorce and gossip. It was probably why Nathaniel had spent a lot of time with his grandpa George and grandma Catherina growing up.

To Benjamin, the incident was a wake-up call. He got his act together and worked hard and grew into a kind and wise soul. But it didn't stop the feelings of discontent he kept hidden behind his ready smile. He left to do his patriotic duty and was surprised that some of the gossip still existed when he returned home.

After he committed to living in Harrison again, he used his friendly manner to welcome people he already knew and to meet new people. His curiosity helped him learn more about a person in fifteen minutes than the person's family would ever know!

He fared better than his siblings anticipated since he had been a rascal with the girls in school. He was well-read and had a good grasp of how to calculate numbers. It was why he loved playing cards … it was a numbers game. But he hated to study and so he didn't.

Over the years, when he heard the tales and whispers about his opinionated sister or his other sister running away from home or Matthew being a freeloader, he would smile, tip his hat, say "good day" and walk away. He was not going to contribute to the hearsay. It didn't mean he was without an opinion, but he wanted to get along with all his siblings.

When he was twenty-five, he had the good fortune of marrying a wealthy farm owner's oldest daughter, Constance Whitley. She was a tall, beautiful blonde, an attractive complement to his six-foot-tall frame and dark hair. Their laughter was infectious, and they had fun during their short courtship. Six months later married. Constance's father had no sons, and his other two daughters had married men who would say all the right things but failed to work hard.

According to his father-in-law, "Laziness is the sin of every farmer. You have to live off the results of your labor and do the right work."

His brothers liked to kid him that he had married a gold-mine of prime property and wealth. Constance's mother's family had grown up on the wealthier side of Chicago and brought money to the Whitley marriage.

Before his pa's stroke, he and his brothers enjoyed talking about their hopes for good crops and what they'd do with the money. Whenever he mentioned his dreams of traveling westward or jumping on one of the locomotives heading east, they'd hoot and holler and call him a gypsy.

He'd smile and continue to dream about the day Constance and he could travel.

As happy as he was, there were days when he heard the distant whistles of the noonday train leaving from the Harrison depot, and his wanderlust would flare-up.

After he had turned thirty, he became the sole beneficiary of his father-in-law's estate. He rejoiced in his good fortune and the acknowledgment of his hard work. His father-in-law believed the best-deserving son inherited from their father, not girls.

Several years later Benjamin lost all four of his children during a flu outbreak. Constance had been devastated and it destroyed her fun-loving personality. He'd been sad too but felt he needed to be strong for her. She'd loved being a mother and that had been her purpose in life. When he mentioned traveling, she looked at him and whispered, "No! I just couldn't. Not with my children gone."

After Constance's pleas, Benjamin allowed his brothers-in-law and nephews to work for him. He believed it was his job as owner of the farm to make sure everyone in the family was well cared for.

Everyone seemed happy until twelve years later, on a cold January morning. Constance awoke fine and healthy, and by nighttime, she was gone. No one knew why. Some said it was from a broken heart.

After Benjamin dried his tears, his only focus became the success of the farm. He had learned that hard work was the best medicine to overcome grief. He wasn't interested in remarrying.

When his two nephews asked for their own parcels of land that spring, he felt that familiar nudging and made them a better offer. The agreement was that they could have the entire farm … home, barn, silos, and land … if they worked for him for seven years. They readily agreed. They did whatever he asked of them the first year and the farm prospered even more. Everyone was happy with the results.

But it was becoming too difficult to keep up the pretense of being a happy farmer. *Is it my time,* Benjamin contemplated? He knew he wanted to travel and see the United States. He read history and geography books during the winter months when there was less to do outdoors.

After his pa's death, he knew it *was time,* especially after his ma declared she was not leaving the old family home. Whenever he thought of his ma, he'd snicker to himself. *With her spunk, I doubt she'll be going anywhere soon. But I must admit she's softened a lot in her older years.*

His siblings became more mired in their version of right and wrong and it grated on his nerves to listen to them speak about each other. It was not how he wished to live his life. Because of his aversion to gossip, he didn't know about the controversy surrounding Matthew until the hours after the burial of his pa. He'd been appalled but decided in that moment that he was done living in Harrison. He had the money and means. It was time to pursue his true goal in life and to leave the family squabbles behind.

He was thankful Matthew had helped their parents keep the Gunther & Sons farm during the devastating Great Depression when so many lost their homes and farms, but had been confused as to why he didn't buy his own farm. He would have helped him with the money if he had asked. He had plenty of it. But he'd learned over the years that Matthew was the type to not ask for help, even when he could use a helping hand. And, offering it would have been an insult to his pride.

Because he was so committed to staying out of the family drama, it never occurred to him to visit Matthew and get his side of the story. Nor did he believe he needed to forgive him. There was nothing to forgive in his mind. *What was done was done. Time to move on.*

It was best to stay out of sight if family members started talking about each other. Otherwise, they would expect him to take sides, and eventually, they'd turn on him.

However, talk about the town and farming community was important to keep him up-to-date on what was happening with farm prices and new laws. So, he only listened until the conversation turned to gossip. Then, he'd bow out.

The full impact of the impending family feud hit home one day over a month later when a neighboring farmer stopped by. He said, "If Maggie is willing to harm Matthew, better be careful what she might do to you." There were no secrets in small towns.

On his forty-fifth birthday, one of his sisters-in-law baked and decorated a cake. As he blew out the candles, he made a silent wish, *Now it's my time.*

Benjamin – 1939 to 1942

The next day, Benjamin drove his 1935 blue Chevy truck into town to talk with Adam and get supplies.

Adam and he had been lifelong friends. Even though Adam lived in town and Benjamin on the farm, they got together as often as they could. Adam had at times put on his farmer's bib overalls and shown up during harvest to help.

Together, Benjamin and Adam drew up a will bequeathing the old Whitley property to his two nephews. In turn, the nephews had to pay the bank monthly over the next six years to finish the mortgage or forfeit the farm and land. In addition, they would pay him a fourth of the profits from crop sales until the mortgage was paid.

Benjamin believed his father-in-law would have been happy for the farm to stay in the Whitley family. His will created a legacy for his nephews' families. He believed the same desire was why his pa felt he had to leave Ohio and travel to Illinois so many years ago. He now understood that passing one's land to the next generation gave meaning to one's sweat and toil.

After he told Adam of his plans to travel, Adam had him sign a power of attorney in the event something happened to him. It gave Adam the legal ability to take care of Benjamin's personal matters. Also, gave him the power to sell the parcel that he'd selected from the Gunther & Sons farm when the price and buyer were right.

The following week, he went to say goodbye to his ma. He also took over boxes of items to be stored in the upstairs attic of the old farmhouse so his nephews wouldn't be tempted to sell the contents for extra cash. He made sure to label each box with Constance's name so he could collect them when he returned home.

His ma had grinned and called him her gypsy after he told her of his intentions. He promised to write her as often as he could.

Then, he went around shaking hands and offering good-byes to his brothers and their families, and Maggie. Nathaniel had moved to Chicago to work as an accountant years after he graduated from college. Benjamin promised Maggie he'd stop in Chicago and have dinner with his nephew before traveling east. He wouldn't have time to visit Rachel and rationalized that with Emma and Susan now living with her, she wouldn't have time to spend with him either.

Finally, after the harvest was done, Benjamin boarded the train north, beaming. He sat and pulled out one of the brand-new spiral notebooks he'd purchased from Maggie's store to start his journal as the conducted boomed, "All aboard!"

There was money in his pocket and money in the bank. Thankfully, being a man allowed him more freedom to travel wherever his spirit wanted to wander, unlike his sister Rachel. He was unaware of her travels but knew she had wanderlust too. They must have inherited it from their pa.

He traveled first to Chicago to visit with Nathaniel. While Nathaniel and he had a good relationship, he would be careful not to become embroiled in the anger Nathaniel felt towards his mother, Maggie.

Nathaniel waited until they were drinking their after-dinner coffee before asking why his mother had divorced his father. Then he said, "She drove my father out of town."

Benjamin said with a sad smile, "I can't answer those questions for you. I'd suggest you ask each of them. Your father is still alive … right? And your grandfather Landes?"

"Well, last I heard from my father, he lived in Boston. I believe my mother said my grandfather died several years ago and was buried in a pauper's grave somewhere. But I've not heard from my father for most of my life. I'd like to know why he left us."

Benjamin gazed thoughtfully at his nephew, marveling at how much he looked like George, Nathaniel's grandpa.

"Will you be traveling to Boston?"

"Maybe, maybe not. I don't know," Benjamin replied with a shrug. "I don't have firm plans."

He paused before continuing, "I just know that your mother loves you. She is the way she is and there is probably a good reason your father felt it necessary to move so far away. You know your grandfather Landes left about the same time. I would ask your father if your mother won't tell you," Benjamin said. He did not want to get in the middle of this quagmire, even if he knew the truth. It was not the way to start off this new chapter in his life with Maggie ragging on him from afar for "telling tales."

Even though Nathaniel persisted in asking questions, Benjamin continued evading them since it wasn't his place to answer them. Then when he was done with his coffee and

Nathaniel had paid the waiter, Benjamin reached out his hand to bid his nephew goodbye.

Benjamin was anxious to get going since he had ordered a hot bath and massage that evening. It'd be his first massage since he was 22.

The next day he jumped on the train in downtown Chicago. He was full of anticipation since today's destination was the northwestern region of Ohio. *Finally!*

The woman last night had taken good care of him. When he'd shared his dilemma about his promise to his pa when he was still in his teens, she said, "Sounds like he never strayed."

Benjamin had roared with laughter. "I believe you're right. My ma would have beaten him with her broom … she's an expert with it."

After the masseuse had also trimmed his nails and hair, he looked and felt like a new man.

Later that night while he lay in the bed, he renounced the promise he'd made to his pa.

It's a burden I no longer wished to carry. I enjoy women, poker, and whiskey. It was ridiculous for the old man to place such a heavy burden on his children to keep the Gunther name from being tarnished. All Pa had to do was write out a will! He'd had 12 years to do it. Now, my siblings are carrying the burden and are mishandling it every step along the way.

He allowed his anger to simmer before falling asleep. The next morning, he put it behind him.

Benjamin

Today's destination was where his parents had begun their marriage in Berlin, Ohio, before joining a wagon train a couple years later to journey to Illinois and follow his pa's dream. He'd heard so many stories that the history and area already felt a part of him.

As the train whistled past various landmarks, he squirmed in his seat from sitting too long on the hard wooden seats. He'd already been up and moving around the train, meeting and talking with other travelers. But the conductor wanted him to stay in his seat and not bother people with his gift for gab. No one had complained. But the conductor felt more comfortable if no one was in his way when he made his rounds up and down the train.

It became a game. When he saw the conductor coming his way, he'd move back to his seat or into an open seat next to the person he was talking with. As the conductor moved past him, he would smile, nod his head, and ask, "How're ya doin'?"

It reminded him of school when the teacher hadn't liked him. He couldn't sit still for long periods of time, mostly due to boredom. So, he would talk to the classmate seated next to him, usually Adam, or squirm to keep awake. The teacher would admonish him, but the teacher didn't win. Neither did his grades, even though he got his work done.

He sat for as long as he could watching the miles of smokestacks spew dark hot ash from the factories. Shaking his head, he marveled at how anyone could stand the smell, having heard that Peter and his sons worked in a similar factory in the Detroit area.

To pass the time, he recalled the Leroy stories his pa told. He got out his notebook and started making notes. Recapturing the stories his pa and ma talked about when speaking of her brothers was important. He hoped to meet them and learn what had happened to them.

From the moment Benjamin stepped off the train in north-western Ohio, he began talking with people. Due to the lateness of the hour, he had to wait until the next morning to check the local courthouse for public deeds. Then, he rented a car to drive out to the area where his grandpa Gunther's farm had been. A few old-timers remembered his parents, his grandpa Henry, and great-uncle Joseph.

Most of the area was not well kept up and was overrun by weeds. It looked like the area had not survived the Great Depression very well. The once-small village of Berlin no longer existed. The only decaying landmarks left were a German Methodist church and graveyard, a fallen down mill, and two boarded-up stores. A couple of large Victorian homes were collapsing too. But there was a bar ... so he spent an hour talking with the mid-day drinkers to learn more about the area.

Then, after several more conversations with locals, he met with some of his pa's nieces and nephews. He heard more Leroy and George stories, many of which he knew were fiction. When he shared the stories his pa and ma had told him, they smiled politely but seemed not to believe him.

He listened to tales about his ma's brothers' scorn of farming. The two brothers also reportedly hated the demands of running a general store near Defiance.

After he drove to Defiance, he sent a telegram to Adam for an introduction to the local banker. He wanted to see if the bank owner knew of the two boys. The banker had never heard of them but was able to show him records of the foreclosure of the store but knew nothing about what had happened to the owners.

No one knew where they had moved. Some believed it was to Virginia. Some thought they took off for Oregon to find gold. During that time, many wagon trains passed through northwestern Ohio and north-central Illinois on their way to cross the big Mississippi River. Thousands of people traveled this route on their way to find their fortune in gold. But it had been long ago, and memories were faulty.

"Many more are broke and living on borrowed time," he remembered his pa saying whenever a farmer wanted to sell and move west. He doubted the brothers had traveled west because there were no stories about them visiting.

For one last time, he traveled back to the German Methodist church graveyard and walked around reading the tombstones. Many of the stones had been weathered to the point the names were forever lost. The church was old and neglected.

He was unable to find the headstones for his ma's Papa Henry and uncle Joseph. There were no family burial sites for Schoenly. There was no record of their burials in the church's records that one of the old-timers kept. He went out to the fallen farms of his grandfather Henry and great-uncle Joseph to see if there were plots there, but there were only hints of the small farms that once existed.

When asked, everyone believed the money his parents had sent for a headstone for Papa Henry was used by the two brothers to buy train tickets and get out of town. It was just before the bank foreclosed on their store and the money owed on both properties.

He questioned whether either of them was alive or had descendants. Again, no one knew. They had both been unmarried. Nothing in the courthouse records indicated anything different about his ma's two younger brothers.

He sighed and felt he had failed his ma.

As an old woman, she would welcome any news about what happened to her birth family. He wrote another letter to say her two brothers—they didn't seem like uncles given their behavior—had left the area. No one had heard from or had reason to hear from either of them ever again.

Next, he decided he'd venture north to upper New York state before the snow began and then move eastward. For the next month, after a day or days, or week or weeks of staying in one place, he'd hop the next train traveling east until he got to the Atlantic Ocean. Then, he boarded a ship in Baltimore to travel north along the Atlantic coast. He had no interest in visiting Nathan, but he did disembark to visit Boston. He would have had to punch Nathan in the nose for how he treated his sister and nephew if he saw him. It would have also been revenge for getting him involved in the whole sordid mess.

He wrote long weekly letters to his ma filled with stories and other details about what he saw. After traveling on different ships sailing north, he went south along the United States coast. He would stay in special places along the way that called to his heart. In his letters home, he wrote of the ocean, freighters, and seashells. He also shared observations about vineyards, factories, and other places where hard-working people earned a living during WWII.

Since he had a gift for listening to others tell their stories, he learned a lot. *Maybe I'll write a book someday,* he mused.

Catherina would read these letters out loud during family Sunday meals at the old farmhouse with pride. The messages gave them insight into places they would never visit and learn about areas of the United States they had never heard of. Since they rarely knew where he would be next, they didn't write letters in response. Once in a while they would receive a telegram and respond immediately. It was usually at Easter or Christmas or their ma's birthday.

Catherina carefully saved every letter she received in an old cigar box for her son. He never found the Schoenly brothers. He believed they had changed their names, didn't leave behind any children, or were no longer alive.

The letters came weekly until the summer of 1942, when they suddenly stopped.

Adam - 1942

After a month without a letter, Catherina worried that something bad had happened and asked Magdalena to find out.

Maggie had said, "Let's wait and give it time. You know the mail doesn't always come like it should." She didn't know what to do and didn't want to admit it.

Then Catherina made the same request of Jacob a few days later. He shrugged. "I wouldn't know where to begin to look," he told his mother.

"How about with Adam?" Catherina asked.

"When I get a chance, I'll ask him," Jacob had replied as he hurried out the door.

"Where would we begin?" Jacob had asked Charlie the following day.

Charlie had shrugged his shoulders. "I know it would mean a lot for Ma to know," Charlie said, before adding, "I'd like to know too." They both agreed.

While everyone was pondering what to do, Rachel took charge after receiving a short letter from Maggie about Benjamin's disappearance.

She contacted Adam and asked him as Benjamin's executor to investigate. Since Adam had grown up in the banking community, his father had contacts along the east coast. He made inquiries. Three months later, posters were mailed and displayed in banks along the east coast from Maine to Florida where the bank owners were friends of Adam's father.

Everyone hoped Benjamin would show up on someone's doorstep—somewhere, anywhere—yet deep down they feared the worst.

No one heard from him again.

Three years later, Adam sold his lifelong friend's farm after the nephews declared they were unable to make the mortgage payments. Adam put on his banker's hat and declared a foreclosure. He used his power of attorney and sold the farm.

He deposited the net proceeds into Benjamin's savings account, minus missing mortgage payments and bank charges.

When the nephews demanded the monies from the sale for themselves, Adam declined. It had nothing to do with the circulating gossip in the community saying they didn't deserve it. It was because it was the right thing to do.

Many were surprised the nephews lost their grandfather's prize. But the truth was, they had relied upon their uncle Benjamin to make all the decisions and didn't know how to run a farm without being told when and how to do things. They had bickered amongst themselves for too long. Eventually, the farm fell into neglect due to the controversy and blame.

Adam had shaken his head. *There were no winners.*

After he sold the old Whitley farm, Adam renewed his search for Benjamin. He felt guilty he hadn't done more sooner but didn't want to encroach on his friend's life. There was so much to tell him. Most importantly, he wanted to hear from his lifelong friend that he was okay.

Due to Rachel's continued, adamant insistence and offer to pay, Adam finally used the money in Benjamin's bank account to hire an investigator to find Benjamin.

Adam used the last letter that had been postmarked in Jacksonville, Florida in May 1942, as the place to start. But the investigators failed to find him, even after backtracking and using the locations shared in his former letters.

After seven long years of hoping and praying, Rachel and her siblings learned Adam had had Benjamin declared dead. He'd been given Catherina's blessing before doing so. None of his siblings learned what had happened.

PART 6

Never let them know how you feel;
they'll use it against you.

Catherina – April 30, 1950

Catherina scooted her tiny, frail body forward on the worn wooden seat, tapping her foot around until she found the stool. She steadied herself by holding onto the side of the checkerboard lacquered table to move off the rocker. Slowly, she stood on the oak floor, scarred from many years of wear.

As she turned around, she noticed the sun had come back out to chase away the dark spring storm clouds. She shifted the old wooden rocker inch by inch for a better view of the back yard and its back forty acres and the freshly turned field of dirt. Someone had been plowing this morning in preparation for spring planting until the thunderstorm chased the tractor back into the barn. She climbed back onto the rocker. It took too much strength to do anything else. Forgotten was the need to add more wood to the stove.

She shivered as she fumbled to adjust the faded, red afghan that had slipped down onto the seat of the rocker behind her. The soft wool throw had been handmade from the sheep on Jacob's farm had been mended often; yet still, it did its job. Her daughter-in-law, Melinda, Charlie's wife, had crocheted it for her as a Christmas gift years ago. While she appreciated having it, she never used it as a wrap or shawl.

Melinda, being wise, several times weekly refolded the afghan throw and draped it over the back of her rocker to pad the back. She didn't say a word about Catherina's not using it as a shawl. It was an unspoken game they both played, a silent way of saying they cared for one another. There were no hurt feelings.

Catherina didn't like change. While some long-ago memories felt like they had just happened yesterday, other memories became foggy. It was devastating since they had become her solace during the many hours and days of living alone. She rocked, reliving the memories that now had turned into regrets.

As Catherina rocked, she examined her hands. The large blue veins stood out from the papery skin. These hands had built this home, her "little field" which had grown into an acre of produce each year and transformed the Gunther & Sons farm into a showplace years ago. They had also picked their share of apples, peaches, and cherries in the orchard. Now they hurt from being crippled and her fingers were knotted with arthritis. They hurt just to look at them.

She sighed as she watched the weather change once again. The wind had picked up. As the sunshine move across the old wood floor, she watched the new storm clouds gather and shadow the barn and farmland outside.

In the sunlight playing across the walls, she noticed that the old wallpaper had faded and peeled. Even though she'd mixed flour and water into a paste to stick the paper back on the wall, it didn't last.

Pfft … wallpaper … such an extravagance.

She'd protested when Magdalena insisted the old brown and white walls needed to be freshened up and informed Catherina that a man she'd hired would be arriving to put it up, probably so the house wouldn't be an embarrassment to her in town. Then, she expected to be reimbursed for his labor. Why it mattered to her, Catherina had no idea since people from town rarely came to visit anymore.

Magdalena should be here soon to check in on me. When it's her turn, she always comes whenever it best suits her, unlike my sons and their wives who live close by. They arrive right at 9 a.m., after completing their morning chores, and right at 4:00 p.m., before their evening mealtime. Sometimes they bring leftover food from their noontime dinners.

Scowling, she shivered again, thinking, *Maybe Magdalena will at least stoke the fire.*

She yearned to lie down for a while, but the effort seemed too daunting and the fear of being caught napping during the day by Magdalena too great. Her daughter scolded her whenever she caught her napping in her bed or in the rocker and threatened to use it as evidence that she could no longer live alone. It was insulting to feel that way in her own home!

It's painful to sit for long periods of time. It's painful to lie down. I can't get comfortable, she thought. It is terrible being old with nothing to do except watch the weather.

With her sons and their families, it was a friendly cat-and-mouse game of whether she was just resting her eyes or napping. But no one wanted her to live with them, even though they would ask her to do so out of kindness.

"What would you care?" Catherina had snapped at her oldest daughter on several occasions.

"I don't want you to hurt yourself. If you fell out of that old rocker, no one would be around to help you. We have our own lives to live and cannot always be around when you need one of us," Maggie would retort.

I doubt she's concerned about my well-being, she thought. *Probably more concerned about the amount of work it would take to move me if I died here.*

Then she thought, *I wonder who will inherit the rocker. She'll probably just take an ax to it.* Catherina snickered as she rubbed the old wooden arms of the beloved rocker George had made for her the year they moved there, just as he had promised.

I wonder what happened to my mama's rocker?

Catherina was the only one who called her eldest daughter Magdalena, now that her George had passed on. It had been the name of Catherina's paternal grandmother. Maggie's brothers and sister called her Magdalena when upset with her, being careful to make sure she didn't hear them.

After the "Maggie incident", they did their best to stay out of their sister's way when she got into one of her moods. The divorce decades ago had left her angry at life and at people. Forced to be pleasant when people came into the store, she reserved her upsets for her family.

I think Magdalena's problem is she worked hard to prove she was as good a store owner as any man. Over the years, she's been successful. But she still wasn't considered part of the "town fathers" of Harrison. She wasn't accepted in the women's groups either. But now that she's sold the store and has softened a bit from hanging around other women, she's being accepted more by the townspeople. If only she'd learn to treat her family members with kindness too.

Catherina

Drowsily, Catherina awoke as the grandfather clock chimed once. She couldn't remember if it was half past the hour or 1 p.m. In her daze, a movement of black fur caused her to sit up straighter in the rocker. She heard an insistent meow and leaned over the armrest to look down at Blackie. He had come out from under the checkerboard table, stretching. The latest noise from the last storm had awoken him from his catnap.

"You're a darn cat," she said in a soft voice.

He jumped with feline grace onto the footstool. He sat there staring at her with his dark golden eyes before continuing his climb onto the wooden seat of the rocker where she sat. Because she was now only five-foot-one, her petite body didn't fill up the rocker seat as it once had. It left room for him to sit next to her. From there, he climbed into her lap, black paw by black paw.

Then, with careful precision, Blackie made his way up on the wooden armrest. From there he jumped to the top of the lacquered white and black checkerboard table. George had loved working with wood and had built it too.

She used the table for eyeglasses, newspapers, and her bible. Blackie would strut back and forth across the table and sweep the newspapers off the table and onto the floor. Then, he would sit in the space he'd created and lick his paws to clean his ears before stretching out and purring with a loud rumble.

She leaned back and resumed rocking … *creak* … *creak* … *creak* while rubbing the worn armrests of the rocker.

She thought about George. He had died eleven years ago, in 1939. She had cared for her paralyzed husband herself. Because of Matthew, they were able to keep the farm.

"God. Bless. Him." With a gentle voice, she spoke these words out loud, enunciating each word. She looked at Blackie and he stared back at her. He had the whitest whiskers.

I've got to be prepared for Magdalena's arrival, she thought. *I'm a mother of seven living children. I ran a strict household and worked right alongside everyone. I made sure they were well educated and expected each of them to graduate from high school. All of them did, which was unusual for farm families. I've softened as I've grown older, unlike Magdalena, who has grown more cantankerous. But sadly, my children still remember my strictness and their children remember the childhood stories about having to work from sunup to sundown.*

Pfft! She thought. *That's life on a farm … it didn't hurt of any of them none.*

The grandfather clock struck twice as Catherina braced for the storm that was about to be unleashed inside the house.

Maggie

Maggie slammed the car door. She didn't know at the same moment Blackie dug his back claws into the checkerboard table and used it as a springboard to flee his nemesis.

Her hope was that she wouldn't get too wet and hurried toward the old farmhouse front door. She was moving with care to not slip and fall in the mud. She was too old to fall and gracefully get back up like she did when she was younger.

After she climbed the steps to the farmhouse, she sighed. She used to love the place when everyone lived here together and got along with one another. The Gunther name meant something in the community then. It meant family. She relished the good feelings and had even restored her maiden name and changed her son's last name to Gunther, much to the upset of her son, Nathaniel.

Now the outside looked dilapidated and worn out.

She made a quick knock to announce herself as she burst through the front door. Pausing, she noted even the wallpaper that she'd had redone was peeling and faded. The old farmhouse had become an embarrassment to her.

Then, she noticed her ma rocking back and forth. She looked a little startled by Maggie's loud entrance. They warily eyed one another to gauge the other's mood, then gave each other a quick nod.

She hated having to check on her ma. But since she had retired and sold the general store, her two brothers living in the area and their wives insisted she take her turn. Today was one of those days.

Maggie shivered before realizing the stove needed more wood. She threw some logs in the old stove before hurrying back out into the damp cold to bring in more wood for later, even though Charlie had made sure there was enough wood stacked that morning.

After bending over to deposit the wood, she stood and felt a sense of profound sadness, which she brushed off. It was out of pure orneriness that her ma insisted on living here by herself. It made for a lot of work for her and her two brothers and their families.

Maggie shrugged and thought, *I need to get this over with so I can get back to town. Tonight is my night to host the bridge club. It's taken me decades to finally be welcomed by the townspeople and don't want to mess it up.*

Maggie plastered a smile on her face. "It should be warmer in here soon. I stopped by to be sure you've eaten. There's another storm coming in, so I need to get back to town fast. Is there anything I can get for you?" Maggie asked as she turned on the light.

Why my ma always sits here in the dark, I'll never understand, she thought.

They had installed electricity a couple years ago, as a collective gift to their ma. Not that she deserved it, after what she tried to do tarnish the memory of their pa.

With the lamp light turned on, Maggie glanced at the unwashed dishes left on the sideboard next to the sink. It was only one plate and one teacup and saucer, but she found it distasteful. The teacup had wet tea leaves in it, which she tossed into the crock that held other used tea leaves. She had considered buying her ma the type of tea that came in bags from her store years ago, but she doubted it would be appreciated.

She left the dishes since she was in a hurry to get back to town, and noticed that the old kitchen trestle table hadn't been cleaned either. She glanced inside the icebox to see if there was food in it and was surprised to see a glass bottle of milk.

Hmm ... I wonder what that is for?

"I don't have time for this," she muttered to herself.

While cleaning up after their ma was part of one's job when checking on her, she didn't believe that rule should apply to her. Her home in town was clean and she hired a local woman to come in once a week. A well-cleaned home was part of being accepted into the town's social community. In her mind, housekeeping was below the status she'd worked hard to achieve. But it didn't stop Maggie from judging her own family based on town standards and hoping they didn't embarrass her.

Her anger at her ma had gotten worse after her pa's death. There were times she felt benevolent, like on Sundays after attending a church sermon and feeling good about what the preacher had said. But it never lasted very long. Even after her son Nathaniel stopped calling and writing her, she didn't feel any compassion for the old woman.

She'd put a smile on her face whenever townspeople or farmers and their wives asked about Catherina. When asked, she'd recite the same response: "She's doing well living in the old family home," and change the subject.

As she looked at her ma sitting in her rocker looking old and frail, she felt only anger. As she thought back to that last conversation with Matthew, her anger rose within her all over again. She shook her head to remove the memories.

"I stopped by to see you on my way back into town. I was over visiting with Charlie to get the new radish seeds that Melinda had been raving about to plant this spring," Maggie said loudly, knowing Catherina didn't hear as well as she used to.

Since her mother didn't reply, Maggie continued her monologue.

"I promised Melinda I would stop by to be sure you've eaten. She had to help Charlie round up a couple of sows that got outside their pens. The storm was horrific over at their place. They had wind damage and lots of tree branches scattered about. It looks like you had some wind damage too. It's Jacob's turn tomorrow afternoon. I'm sure he'll check around to make everything is okay."

Maggie continued speaking quickly, "Melinda will be here tomorrow morning, as usual, to help you clean up and eat. Another storm is on the way. It stopped raining long enough for me to stop here before hurrying home."

She glanced around the living room and babbled, "I don't want to stay out here overnight. I'm sure you can find enough to eat. I have plans for tonight, so I got to go." Maggie had intended her words to sound lighthearted. Yet they sounded annoyed, even to her own ears.

Maggie paused for a breath, checked the stove for wood again, and turned on another lamp near her ma. She breathed to calm down her nervousness.

Drat that old woman, Maggie thought. She wasn't used to having a family member make her feel so nervous.

"I hope there's no spring snow with those clouds being so dark. It sure is cold enough, though. Is there anything I can get for you? Are you warm enough?" Maggie chattered, repeating herself, as she checked the bedroom to make sure everything looked okay. She'd stopped expecting a response.

Maggie shook her head as Catherina rocked in her chair as though nothing was said. *She never appreciates anything I do.*

She paused by the radio and contemplated turning it on for her mother's benefit. Catherina enjoyed listening to gospel music.

If she wants it on, she can get up out of that old rocker and do it herself.

Suddenly, Maggie paused and stopped. She turned around and sniffed. *Whew …*

Her Ma hadn't made it to the outhouse again, or the porcelain potty.

Well, I don't have time to change her diaper. If she insists on living here by herself, she can clean herself up. I don't have the time, Maggie thought with anger. *I have more important things to do. I don't have time to be her nursemaid. It'd be best if she moved into one of her sons' homes where it would be easier on everyone. I won't have her living in town with me. I don't want to take care of her.*

She had only been there ten minutes and her frustration was mounting.

We could install an indoor bathroom for her. But it costs money. No one believes she deserves it after what she did after Pa died.

There is no forgiveness, she thought with righteous fervor. *I've never believed her lies about Pa's wishes. Pa would never do that to any of us. He loved us all. Time to get out of here!*

As she left, she yelled back over her shoulder while flipping her hand in goodbye, "Remember to lock your doors. This isn't like the old days. I got to get home before the storm hits. I can't get stuck here. Bye!"

She slammed the front door to make sure it latched.

Maggie's righteousness and anger were her trademarks. Nathaniel refused to talk with her. She had grandchildren who only visited once when they were young and the family had been in the process of moving from Chicago to Los Angeles.

He blamed her for knowing the truth about why his father had abandoned him so long ago and refusing to tell him. The truth was, she didn't know. Even after all these years, no one was talking. She'd suggested he talk with his uncle Benjamin. But he obviously wasn't talking either or she would have heard something by now.

Even having turned 65 earlier in the month, she felt spry and able to go where she wanted. But it didn't occur to her to go and visit her son and his family. The thought of air or rail travel seemed overwhelming and she feared for her safety after reading the daily newspapers about women traveling by themselves. She was always anxious about Rachel's traveling alone when it was time for her annual visit.

Growing old and dying alone didn't cross her mind since she had friends in town and from church to keep her busy. If worse came to worst, she expected her family to take care of her.

Maggie couldn't drive away fast enough to get rid of the demons of hatred she felt. "I'm not responsible for splintering the family apart. Ma did that to us," Maggie whispered out loud.

It never occurred to her that she could become an old woman in an old wooden rocker like her ma. All she could think was her ma had been once a domineering, vibrant woman. Now she was old and alone. It was her ma's fault her life was that way.

Catherina

Catherina heard the slam of the door and was glad the in-door storm had blown out so fast.

Magdalena is old enough to slow down and stop mumbling, Catherina thought with frustration. Watching Magdalena scurry around between the outdoors, kitchen, bedroom, and living room had reminded her of a cat chasing a mouse ... back and forth ... here and there.

She could now relax; it would be three days before Magdalena would return. Charlie and Jacob and their families were much kinder people. While she blamed her eldest daughter for the hateful mess the family now endured, she knew her sons didn't ... they blamed her and Matthew. She didn't know what her youngest daughter Rachel felt since they never discussed it.

It's why I'm alone. It's Maggie's fault no one comes to see me.

She felt her stomach growl and said out loud to Blackie, wherever he was hiding, "I better go and fix some bread and milk for dinner. Do you want some too?"

After she stood up, Catherina spied Blackie's red nose first and then saw him slowly emerge from under a chair. She walked over and slowly stooped down to scratch his ears. She feared that Blackie's life would be cut short after she died, given Magdalena's aversion to cats, but there was nothing she could do about it.

"When I'm gone, you need to find another home. Fast. Before Magdalena finds you," she whispered. "I don't know why she hates cats so much."

Shaken and saddened by Blackie's fear, she returned to her rocker. Forgotten was her growling stomach. After Blackie was nestled in her lap purring, Catherina stayed intent on petting Blackie to soothe him … and herself.

The sun disappeared and the darkness took over.

"Another storm's brewing," she whispered to herself. This time it was outside her old farmhouse and she felt much safer.

Catherina

Blackie snoozed as the rocker moved back and forth, and periodically meowed in his sleep. *A mouse must be chasing him in his dreams,* Catherina grinned.

Catherina thought back to happier times with family. Thanksgiving had been her favorite holiday.

There had been massive dinners of turkeys and hams. Everyone brought a pie—mince, pumpkin, apple, and cherry pies. They had to take a plank of wood and set it across two sawhorses to hold all the homemade goodies.

She had spent days before each big event making homemade bread and gingerbread. Her daughters would mash the potatoes that morning and prepare vegetables and fruits that had been canned during the summer. It was a feast to behold.

Then, after the meal, the kids would play games outdoors and someone would play the piano. Charlie would bring out his violin and everyone sang in their loudest voices … many times off-key. But no one cared. It was a grand time.

George and she would sit smiling and laughing, tapping their fingers on the armrests of the rockers and tapping their feet on the floor. The music swelled their hearts with joy and everyone got along for the day.

I wonder when and where Thanksgiving will be later this year. It's so tiring to enjoy family times together anymore. There are too many people. I don't even recognize who is who and then they get mad at me for not remembering. I wish it could be here … just my children … at least one more time.

She thought about the family troubles. The old stories about Matthew vs. Peter had been replaced by stories about Catherina vs. her children or Matthew vs. his siblings. *I wish they could put all of the conflicts aside. Embrace the spirit of the holidays and of forgiveness, at least for one day.*

They have made way too much of it, Catherina thought as she allowed the tears to roll down her wrinkled cheeks. *I miss the good old days of everyone getting along.*

The week before, she suggested to Magdalena gathering her children and their spouses—without grandchildren or great-grandchildren—to celebrate Thanksgiving. Magdalena responded, "I have enough things to do without taking on more work!"

She went on to say in a patronizing tone, "Stop blaming us for you being all alone. No one will forgive you if you don't ask for forgiveness. It's your fault our family no longer is a whole family."

Catherina had stared at her daughter in shock, wondering when she had become so righteous and pious.

How am I to blame? They've become judge and jury without listening to the truth of George's wishes. The land and farm are George's and mine to do with as we please. We're the ones that labored and did the hard work. Now they've dishonored it and us for their beliefs that what is ours should be theirs! All these judgmental fools and I bore them! George expected me to fulfill his promise to Matthew because he was unable to do it himself. I just don't know how to fix it. A mother's greatest regret is her children not getting along. No one seems to care enough to step up and do the right thing.

Blackie decided at that moment to open his eyes and stand up to stretch. After completing a small circle on the wooden seat of the rocker, he sat back down. Then, he placed his paws on her lap and looked up at her.

She petted him absentmindedly, while gazing at the piano.

No one had played it in so many years. She considered giving it to Nathaniel, who used to love to play on his many visits. But he was too busy with his own life—and too angry at his mother.

The truth was, Nathaniel still blamed his mother for the split. Whatever happened, his father and grandfather Landes, the preacher, had been so ashamed they ran away in the middle of the night.

Yet giving Nathaniel something would upset the others. Even though they wouldn't want the piano. Also, they still blamed Nathaniel for his angry attitude toward his mother. "He needs to get over it," his aunts and uncles would say. So much judgment! She shook her head at the irony of it all.

I wonder where he inherited that from?

She looked at the child's rocking chair that sat next to the piano. George had made this gift for Magdalena's first Christmas in Illinois. But Magdalena considered it an eyesore and didn't want it in her home. To Catherina, it was a beautiful memory of a happier time.

She decided that the next time Matthew came, she'd give it to him. Magdalena would only give it to someone to buy their loyalty.

Family isn't supposed to treat each other that way. Supposedly, blood held the family together.

She closed her eyes and allowed her gnarled fingers to gently rest on Blackie's warm fur. As she relaxed, she nodded off.

Catherina – May 2, 1950

While she waited for Maggie to arrive, her eyes scanned the wall of family photographs that dated to 1910. She'd pulled them from an album and hung them in the living room. In the growing darkness, she could only feel the images she had etched in her heart as a mother and grandmother.

When she was younger, their home had been the pride of the community. The farming and town community had always felt invited and welcomed. She wondered when it became a bigger mark of success to live in town and not on a farm. Why were townspeople considered more important than farm people? Why did farm people feel townspeople needed to approve of them in order to be considered worthy?

George had been a farmer and during the winter evenings would build many things. She gazed at the plant stand with the Christmas cactus sitting on it. The red and white blooms had burst forth during Easter this year. She smiled when she spotted the marble railroad. She had spent hours watching her children and grandchildren place marbles at the top and watch the marbles roll back and forth down the rails to the bottom.

She thought, *I need to make sure and give these to Matthew before I die.*

In her heart, she knew he deserved more, after all his hard work keeping this farm going for so many years. Matthew's siblings wouldn't agree, but if she didn't give them to Matthew, he would never get anything.

She missed her family and didn't like living alone. The noise and people running in and out had given her life meaning. She'd felt alive and worthy to have so many children and a prosperous farm. Yet, her eighty-three years of age and staunch independent German pride would not allow her to be a burden on anyone. So she continued to live alone and would challenge anyone saying otherwise. *I don't need help; I can get by on my own.*

Never let them know how you feel, she remembered her Papa Henry saying to her when her mama passed. *They'll use it against you. She hadn't understood it at the time. Now, sadly, it made too much sense.*

She refused to ask forgiveness from her children and didn't believe she needed to do so. Nor had she asked for forgiveness from Matthew for doing what she had had to do. Everyone blamed her for being an old woman and not knowing what she was doing. But she'd done her best to honor her husband's wishes. Sadly, everyone believed she had defied her husband's legacy.

I can only do what I can do. I had no other choice, Catherina reminded herself. *I hope God and George forgive me.*

It never occurred to her that George should have been the one asking her and his children for forgiveness—especially Matthew. If he had honored his promise in writing, this controversy would not have occurred.

PART 7

*Time doesn't wait for someone to honor
their promise, and doesn't erase the
importance of a promise made.*

Maggie – July 5, 1939

Maggie felt sick to her stomach as she locked up the general store right at 6:00 p.m. just like she did every night, except on Sundays or holidays. On the Sabbath, everything was closed, except for the churches.

As the eldest child, she had taken care of Matthew and Charlie, the youngest.

Even with a 14-year difference between Matthew and her, they had grown the closest. He would tease her like little boys do. She had made sure she gave him special treats on baking day. One of his favorites had been bread with cinnamon and sugar sprinkled on it. They took walks late in the day after all the chores were done or sat on a tree stump in the woods and made-up funny stories.

Their easy comradery changed when she started dating her husband-to-be, Nathan Landes. There weren't many good men in town to choose from and she didn't want to be the only girl in her high school graduating class not getting married, so Maggie set her sights on him.

His family had moved into town the previous year and his father was the new preacher at the Methodist church. Her family had attended off and on over the years, mostly for christenings, weddings, and funerals.

Nathan's father was enterprising and had bought the local general store from a man wanting to move north. Since Nathan had stopped going to school in 10th grade, he was expected to take over running the store and to marry. His father didn't believe in idle hands, no matter how wealthy your family was.

Maggie liked Nathan's good looks and dark wavy hair, and the fact he lived in town. His family had money. Marrying a boy from town would elevate her status in the community, especially marrying a store owner. He had succumbed to her chasing him and was courting her. She feared that one of her brothers would say something about her outspoken ways and he would be no longer want her as his wife. He was her only option to get off the farm and out from under her ma's demands.

One day Nathan had surprised her by coming out to visit in the early afternoon. While they walked and talked, four-year-old Matthew, careful not to be seen, followed them. Then, just as Nathan attempted to kiss her, Matthew had jumped out and yelled, "Boo!"

Maggie was startled and hadn't known what to do in that moment. Normally she would yell at him. But knew that wasn't possible with Nathan standing right there staring at her. As she swallowed her anger with a smile plastered on her face, she watched as Nathan's facial expressions changed from a smile to surprise to resignation. She became uncharacteristically quiet. She'd hoped this was the moment he asked her to marry him.

Instead of kissing her, he smiled again. After glancing back at Matthew staring at them, he murmured, "I better get back into town and help my father at the parsonage."

As soon as he left, she feared he would never ask since he wasn't an assertive guy.

Furious, she ran around looking for Matthew who had fled when Nathan did. As soon as she saw him hiding behind the willow tree, she started yelling at him for the damage he'd done. She'd stooped to pick up a small branch from the willow tree to use as a switch, even though their pa had never taken a switch to any of them.

She swung the branch over his head screaming, "I don't want you anywhere near me. Ever again!"

He cowered on the ground.

Hearing the commotion, George and Catherina had come running to see what was happening.

When they arrived, George grabbed the switch from Maggie's hand. At the same time, Catherina, all 5' 3", stooped over and picked up her son to hug him to her. She glared at Maggie like a mama bear protecting its cub.

George commanded quietly said with a strong edge to his voice, "Take him."

After about ten yards, Matthew had squirmed out of Catherina's hold and run into the barn.

In the meantime, George, with a firm grasp on Maggie's upper arm, dragged her away from the barn and farmhouse and towards the farm lane that led to the backfields.

"What was that?" George asked with anger in his voice, shaking at what he'd just witnessed.

"You wouldn't understand," Maggie rasped out through her tears and anguish. She stared defiantly out to the backfields where Jacob, Peter, and Benjamin were picking up stones to clear another field.

"Tell me."

Maggie just shook her head. She didn't know what to say.

They'd stopped in the clearing. George kept his hand firmly holding his eldest daughter's arm.

"No boy or man is worth coming between you and your family. Never again will you treat family that way," George stated angrily. "Or … I'll … take this …" He held up the switch he'd grabbed from her and threw it. They watched as the brown collie dog chased after it.

He let go of her arm and walked back to see how Matthew was doing, shaking his head in anger.

When he returned, he saw Catherina telling a story to Rachel and Charlie who were seated on the ground at her feet. She was perched on an upturned wooden bucket just inside the big barn door with straw scattered about that had been spilled when cleaning the horse and pony stalls earlier in the day.

"Where's …?" George asked Catherina after he'd calmed down and could talk.

Catherina nodded towards the barn where Matthew had gone to seek comfort near one of the ponies. A couple of cats and the yellow collie dog lay next to him, surrounding them.

"I've never …" George stared as he started to speak with a tear in his eye. Catherina could only nod sadly.

After seeing Matthew was okay, George patted Catherina's shoulder and walked over to saddle up a horse. He said to Catherina as he rode out of the barn, "I'll go see how the three boys in the backfield are doing. If they've gathered up enough rock, we can start building the stone fence in the back. We'll be back before sundown."

Catherina nodded and brushed away a tear from the corner of her eye. She'd been scared too and had never seen Maggie so angry. She stood and shooed Rachel and Charlie into the house for a nap, then woke Matthew up to join them. He straggled behind with straw clinging to his clothes and rubbed his tear-stained face as he looked around to make sure it was safe.

After her pa had left her, Maggie hung her head and toed the dirt. She was still upset over what had happened. She walked with her head down to the stump where Matthew and she shared happy moments together. The brown collie dog had brought the stick back to her but dropped it and stretched out at her feet, panting.

She felt the loss deep in her heart and her tears refused to stop flowing. It was terrible to feel so helpless about what to do with graduation so close. She had no desire to work outside the home or continue living under her parents' roof. It felt like her hopes died when Nathan left in a hurry. Her heart hardened against the little boy who had robbed her of her future.

As the sun moved from the south of the west, she realized her deepest fear was that no man would ever want her. No one came by to court her, even though she was one of the better-looking girls in the community and a Gunther. Her reputation for being outspoken was well known in the small community of Harrison and scared many young men and most young women.

A little while later, she looked up to see her ma beckoning her. "Looks like it'll rain tomorrow. We need to finish getting the garden in." Catherina handed over her straw hat and hoe. Maggie nodded and donned the hat.

Her ma's little field had expanded from half an acre to a full acre in order to feed everyone after the last three kids were born. They used stakes and string to mark off the rows and mark the seeds being planted.

Rachel came out a little later to help. They were making progress when Charlie and Matthew came out to help after waking from their naps. When Matthew spotted Maggie, he ran to the barn. Catherina nodded to Charlie to help her plant squash and watermelons, while she sent Rachel to see where Matthew was. She came back saying, "He found the new kittens."

"Leave them be," Catherina said. "You don't want their mama to leave them."

After the seeds were nestled deep in their hills of soil, Catherina joined Rachel, Charlie, and Matthew to watch the kittens. Maggie continued working to finish up the rows and planting. When she was done, she removed her straw hat and wiped her brows with a handkerchief. After surveying the work done, she sighed, exhausted. She placed her hoe back in the shed, and she and the brown collie went back to the stump under the shade of the old willow tree.

Later after Pa and her brothers returned from the field, Rachel and Charlie raced over to her and laid some wild-flowers at her feet. They said in unison, "Time for dinner" and raced back to the house. She stood and followed them to the farmhouse. Instead of joining the family, she walked upstairs to the bedroom she shared with Rachel, undressed and washed, before crawling into bed, where she stayed until morning.

Three days went by. Jacob said to his pa, "Do you know Matthew's been having nightmares? He insists on crawling into one of the boys' beds. It's Maggie's job to look after him."

George shrugged and said, "Let him be and let him sleep with you and your brothers."

Jacob shrugged and shook his head. It was women's work. But knew better than to say anything because he could feel the tension in the air.

George and Catherina weren't sure what to do about Maggie. She'd graduated from high school over a week ago. It was impossible for her to continue living at home after the incident with Matthew. They talked about who in town would give her a job since she had a knack working with numbers.

As they sat in their rockers side by side watching their two youngest sons play with the marble railroad, Maggie came flying into the room, having met with Nathan in town.

Matthew had done a crab walk to scoot to the other side of the marble railroad, a move that did not escape his parents' notice.

"I'm getting married to Nathan in the fall, after harvest," Maggie announced, dancing around.

Catherina and George glanced at each other, surprised but pleased. Then Catherina said, "Why don't you get married on July 4th? The same day we got married."

Maggie stopped dancing and looked at them with a bemused expression, noticing that they both looked towards Matthew. She said, "But people will say it's a shot-gun wedding getting married so fast." She feared the gossip of townspeople since she needed to fit in.

George asked her, "Is it?"

Maggie adamantly shook her head no.

Catherina spoke up, "Then don't worry about it."

Maggie and Nathan married and moved into the Victorian house on south Main Street that his father had bought them as a wedding gift. She enjoyed having her own home and working in the general store with Nathan. But despite her happiness, her heart didn't open again to Matthew. Her pride wouldn't allow someone who had threatened her future to be trusted. In her mind, "That was that!"

Matthew slowly became like his old self again, except he still feared speaking up and when someone would raise their arm, he'd flinch and move away.

Maggie and Matthew never forgot that moment. Over the years, she came to regret that horrible afternoon, but she still believed Matthew should ask for her forgiveness since it'd been his fault for scaring Nathan off.

Maggie – July 6, 1939

While she had been the one to suggest to her pa that Matthew help her parents back in 1927, it was because Matthew's poverty had become an embarrassment. Townspeople or farmers would ask about him when they came into the store. She would smile and say, "He's fine." They would comment about Matthew working for Smythe, and say they hoped Matthew got his money from the old miser.

Now, a dozen years later, Maggie felt betrayed for a second time by her brother, who had not appreciated what she'd done but who wanted to keep everything for himself. What he had done was unforgivable and he would pay for his deceit.

Maggie knew what needed to be done. She had fretted all night long thinking it over. As soon as Lucille arrived at the store, Maggie hurried out to her auto. She had to get out to Jacob's farm to see him before anything else happened.

As she drove, she thought about her ex-husband's move back to Boston, where he had been born. Nathan's father left the same day his son did. Neither returned. Neither sent a letter or an apology. Nothing.

It had been depressing never knowing what had happened. Her pa had stepped in and handled everything. But he'd refused to tell her the details, saying, "It's better you don't know. It's too gruesome to talk about. Stay focused on your son and that store."

He made sure she had a divorce and the store and title to the house were hers. His focus was on protecting her and his grandson as much as possible, given that she was only 29. Still, she had to gain acceptance from the townspeople of Harrison on her own merit and not rely on the Gunther name. At first, she'd been resentful of the pressure, but now she was thankful she'd done it on her own. She had insisted on keeping the store, even though her pa had advised her to sell it.

The only person she believed knew about the situation was Benjamin after his behavior that Sunday when she and Nathaniel came to stay at the family home the day after Nathan left. But the two of them never spoke about it.

Her anger at Matthew for trying to steal her pa's farm kept her vigilant during the five-mile drive out to Jacob's farm. *The thief. Wait until I tell everyone what he is trying to pull.*

Keeping her eyes fixed on the road, she was going as fast as she dared. The old farm roads were difficult and rutted. It would be a waste of precious time if she needed to get a local farmer to pull her out of the ditch.

Oops … she missed hit a large pothole, almost ending up sideways in the ditch.

Slow down, she reminded herself as she eased up on the gas.

The thought brought a sad smile to her face. Her admonishment sounded like her pa when she was younger and trying to do her chores too fast.

One time she had attempted to gather eggs as fast as she could. The chickens in the coop threatened to gang up on her. There had been a fox living in the area. When hearing all the ruckus, pa hurried out with his rifle to see what was going on, afraid the sly critter had returned. The only sly one he found was his daughter. They had a good laugh and he called her the fox girl.

Jacob was the only brother she felt comfortable talking to since he was the oldest son and she was the eldest child. He was the best choice to pull their siblings together for the impending fight.

"How dare Matthew think he can get away with this? There are six of us and only one of him," she said out loud.

Maggie knew her brothers didn't like her assertive style. They felt embarrassed by her divorcing Nathan, whom they believed had been their friend. Divorce went against their religious beliefs, especially those of Jacob and Charlie. Because Nathan had left so fast without saying goodbye, they didn't know who to blame.

She considered her mild-mannered sister and sisters-in-law. They often didn't talk about difficult topics either. They'd talk about the weather, canning, mundane things. As a female store owner, she had challenges they couldn't understand, and she had no interest in their daily activities.

Jacob and Maggie – July 6, 1939

When she finally arrived at Jacob's farm, she saw him out in the field. He'd bought a new tractor before their pa's death and was pulling an empty wagon behind him. Even though his sons now farmed the property and did the hard work, Jacob was still in charge.

She stopped, threw the car into park, and jumped out. She ran out into the field yelling after him to stop, waving her arms, chasing him as he moved away from her. The problem was, she had forgotten to dress for the farm.

As she stopped and tried to brush the dust coming from behind Jacob's tractor and wagon from her dress, she felt a pull on her nylon hose. A nettle had caused a run.

Slow down, she reminded herself. After pausing to breathe, she yelled again at Jacob to stop.

You know how Jacob hates any sign of emotion. You have more hosiery at home.

After he braked and moved the gear into idle, she walked up to the front side of the tractor, in front of the big right wheel. She screamed over the sound of the engine while trying to gather her breath, "Matthew. Has. Done. It!"

Jacob looked down at his oldest sister, her hair disheveled and dust clinging to her clothes. He thought, *What's gotten into her so early in the day?*

He shut down the tractor to save gas, thinking, *This may take a while. She sure didn't dress for the occasion.*

"He's trying to steal the farm, our inheritance," she shouted again after the engine noise stopped. A couple of tears worked their way down her dusty face.

Jacob sat stunned by her words. He looked down at this sister from his tractor seat and shook his head in disbelief.

"Why would you say that? He's been working the land there for many, many years. Why would you think that he's stealing it?" Jacob asked calmly. He scratched his balding head under his cap as he looked around. *I don't have time for her hysterics with so much to do.*

We all agreed to wait until after the harvest before addressing the issue of the will and their pa's wishes. Now she's causing all this ruckus. Over what? We still have a couple months before harvest time.

Maggie yelled through her tears, "It's been twelve years. Because he told me so."

Jacob didn't like it when Maggie exaggerated. He looked over to the adjacent field. The green leaves of his corn crop looked good, and he felt pride in all that he accomplished with his sons and family.

He glanced at the wood loaded in another wagon located next to the barn. It needed unloading before noon and he needed to get the wagon he was pulling loaded with wood too. When he looked back down at his sister again, he had a scowl on his brown, weathered face. He pushed his flat cap further back on his head showing a brown and white farmer tan line.

Jacob sighed and stayed calm as he said, "I don't know what you said that would cause him to say such nonsense. I'll talk with him if you'd like me to." He was hoping that would appease her. His wife, Merry, had reminded him at breakfast there was some type of church event that evening.

Maggie continued, "Matthew walked in while I was talking with Ma. That's what he said. The farm was his after all these years of farming it."

Matthew was not the type to lie, thought Jacob. But he was stunned.

He and his brothers had talked about how they would divide the farm after their pa died. They joked about which son would receive which parcel of land. Of course, the coveted acreage with the most fertile soil was the area Matthew cleared during the time he'd been living and working there.

Then he remembered that Matthew hadn't been part of those conversations. He'd been busy working. He only came to family events on holidays. By an unspoken agreement, no one ever talked about the farm during those get-togethers. Mostly they didn't want to say anything about Matthew and his family being freeloaders. They wanted to avoid another scene and aftermath like the time when Peter was the overseer.

The brothers had talked about their parents' kindness in letting Matthew and his family live in the tenant's home. Jacob knew that Matthew hadn't liked working for Smythe, feeling that he wasn't getting his fair share. But it had been a sudden move for him to leave there and move into the tenant home the same day Peter vacated it.

Jacob and his two remaining brothers, Benjamin and Charlie, had always agreed. "What did you expect from Smythe, a miserly old coot?"

But that didn't make the Gunther & Sons farm Matthew's.

Where would he get such an idea? Must be from living there so long, Jacob thought.

He also knew that if it wasn't for Matthew, the family farm might not have survived after their pa's many strokes. He and his brothers would grudgingly admit this to themselves when Peter wasn't around. They hadn't forgotten about all the complaining and work they had to do when Peter lived there and was the overseer. He was glad that Peter was no longer in charge of manipulating them into doing his work.

It was also good that Matthew could get along with their ma due to his easygoing style.

Of course, the brothers thought there should only be a five-way split of the family property. But due to Maggie's divorce and Rachel's being a spinster, that wasn't going to happen. Their heritage demanded they take care of them, even though their sisters' bank accounts probably contained more money than the rest of theirs put together!

In addition, the brothers did not want problems like those their uncle Leroy had caused for their pa. They'd heard those stories so many times over the years they knew them by heart.

Too opinionated, like her mother, he thought, *looking down at Maggie. Now, look at what she's done. I thought we were going to wait.*

Sighing, Jacob asked Maggie, "Well, what are you going to do about it?"

She looked up at him with outrage. "Me? What am I going to do about it? Thanks for your help."

Slow down ...

She replied with a hard edge to her voice, "I don't need you to patronize me. I went over to get Ma to sign her will bequeathing the 500 acres to us. Equally. Like we had talked about a couple of weeks ago after Pa's funeral."

Maggie taunted him, "Did you know she owns it ... all of it ... her name is the only name on the deed?!"

She recognized his shock. The news dazed him.

"Wha—?" he stammered. "How did that happen?"

Maggie hurried on as if he hadn't spoken. "Someone had to do it. Clearly, you don't have what it takes to get it done," she said before turning and walking away. She was seething.

Just like a man to blame it on a woman. I'm going to get Ma to sign that damn will and show them I'm smarter than they are.

Someday they'll thank me.

Maggie – July 7, 1939

The next day at noon, Maggie had Clyde take over the store since it was Lucille's day off. As she was leaving, she looked around the store with pride. It had taken years after her former husband left to bring back customers.

Maggie had gotten another copy of the will from Adam a few days before. He had reminded her that there could be no intimation. She smiled in agreement, not voicing her true thoughts: *She will sign this thing now or else.*

Her plan was to arrive when she believed Matthew would be out in the fields or having his mid-day dinner at home. She planned to park alongside the farmhouse, so the barn hid her auto from Matthew's view.

After she parked the car, she looked around to make sure Matthew wasn't close by. She found her ma seated under the old willow tree, snipping the last of the green beans for canning.

What was the stool doing outside? She'll ruin it in that damp grass. Pa had made it for the piano.

Slow down. Calm down. Breathe.

Maggie walked over to her. She smiled to keep her face from showing her annoyance, but that didn't last long.

She watched as the snips from each end of the green string beans landed either in the bushel basket or on the ground. They would make good hog feed later.

Catherina stiffened when she saw Magdalena's shadow and realized her daughter was standing over her. She hadn't heard her car.

She breathed and rested her hands on the metal pan holding the snipped string beans before looking up at her daughter. Not surprisingly, she saw a scowl on her daughter's face. Mentally she prepared herself for a verbal onslaught.

Maggie toed a couple of the fallen snips lying on the ground. She focused on moving them away from the bushel basket before saying anything.

Be calm, she reminded herself. *Slow down. Remember, Adam told you this wouldn't be easy. But he wasn't aware of any promise made by George and Catherina to Matthew. He was sure Rachel would have mentioned it. Or Charlie, with whom he had played poker the night before.*

But—he cautioned her—Matthew might have something in writing. If he did, Adam would be unable to represent the family. He wasn't going to get in the middle of any controversy due to his relationships with the family.

She had been so determined to be kind when she arrived. All those intentions fell to the wayside when she noticed her ma cringing at the sight of her.

Maggie's face turned red in shame and fueled her anger.

"How dare you try to steal this place from all of us children?" She spoke in as quiet of a tone of voice she could muster. She looked around to be sure no one could hear her.

"We're all your children. We did our share of work growing up. This farm belongs to all of us. Not just Matthew," Maggie continued.

Catherina said, "I didn't …"

Maggie continued as if her mother hadn't spoken. "Pa would have never agreed to allow this to happen. He loved all of us. Not just Matthew."

After she was silent for a moment, with tears in her eyes, Catherina responded with a soft quiver in her voice. "Yes. He did love each of you. But none of you were able or willing to live here and take care of us. Matthew, Grace, and their children did."

After a short pause, Catherina started to say, "Your pa …"

Maggie cut her off with the same stern voice and waved her hands as she spoke, with the pages of the will fluttering in the breeze. "That's all nonsense. We have all been available to help you. But we have our own families and lives." She caught herself before adding, *and no one could do it exactly right, according to your standards.*

Using the toe of her shoe, she kicked at some of the snips and sent dirt flying past the bushel basket.

Catherina thought back to the times she had asked for help from her children—usually, without success. She had begged them to come help her, for their pa's sake. She had a to-do list ready and waiting for them. During monthly Sunday dinners, she learned to sneak in her requests.

Instead of relying on her family, she paid neighbor girls and boys to help. Their parents needed the money. She was kinder to them than her own family because they were thankful for her kindness.

Sometimes Matthew and his daughters would help if she asked during a time when they weren't busy doing other things. That stopped after her granddaughters told Grace she was paying others, but not them.

Maggie continued with an edge in her voice, "I spoke with my brothers and we're not going to stand for it." The tears that had threatened to spill had stopped. She had gotten a firm control of her anger.

Even though she had only spoken to Jacob, she knew her mother wouldn't know the difference. Neither would Matthew. She and her brothers would stick together on this matter. Rachel could be a problem since Matthew was her favorite brother. But there were more of them believing the farm belonged to all of them.

"He can have his share, but that's all. He and his family should be thankful they had a place to live all these years," Maggie stated with deliberate slowness. She wanted to make sure her ma understood her determination to do the right thing.

Before Catherina could respond, Maggie threatened, "We'll take it to court. I've talked with Adam."

Again, before Catherina could respond, Maggie remembered to ask, "You don't have it in writing, do you?"

Maggie prayed she knew the answer to this one. She stood with her fingers crossed hidden by the papers, praying for the right answer. Adam had cautioned her that it would be an uphill battle if George had left a separate written document.

"Your pa promised Matthew the farm," Catherina whispered.

Maggie didn't hear her. She was focused on controlling her anger while fidgeting to keep a lookout for Matthew, hoping to avoid another scene. She wasn't afraid of him. But she didn't know if Matthew had hired some workers to help him today.

The fear of being overheard and having Adam hear about it made her cautious. She had her reputation to uphold.

Maggie was growing impatient.

This time Catherina whispered in a louder tone of voice, "No, we didn't think we needed to. Your pa didn't think we needed to do so since it was being kept in the family after I passed."

Catherina's sadness was turning into anger. "We should be able to do what we want with our money and property. It was your pa's. Now it's mine. Not yours!"

Maggie hissed, "You can't. It's ours and we will make sure we get it all."

She stormed away, taking the will with her. She was angrier than when she first arrived, if that was even possible. It was too bizarre. How could her own ma and brother do this to hurt all of them?

How could this be happening in my family? Adam had shared that many families had problems. Many times, they were poor and had nothing else to count on. Many wealthy families had a similar dilemma when their children believed they were owed more than their siblings.

We're upright citizens and attend church. What would the town and farm community say when they heard about this? I hope it doesn't hurt my store. Or the Gunther name.

This wasn't right.

She vowed to try again tomorrow after she calmed down, if she could.

Matthew – July 8, 1939

The next day Matthew noticed Maggie's car parked alongside the farmhouse again. He'd seen it there yesterday, but the car was gone before he could get there.

Today, he experienced a bad gut reaction. He didn't trust Maggie. No one parked there. He knew Maggie was causing trouble about the farm. But he wasn't sure how to handle it. He knew he needed to find out. Over the past few days, he'd hoped that without any Maggie sightings, this nightmare had stopped.

He directed his team of workhorses to the edge of the field and under a tree as fast as he could without spooking them. Dropping the reins, he walked as fast as he could in his work boots to the farmhouse.

As he entered, he wiped his face with a handkerchief. Maggie looked up at him as he entered with a winning smile on her face. She had heard him wipe his work boots at the door and was prepared for him.

"She signed it and I'm in charge. I'm the executor of her will. All the brothers agreed." Maggie beamed.

"You and your family can continue to live here until after harvest. Then you need to stop freeloading off your ma. Get your own place like the rest of us have done," Maggie dictated.

Matthew looked at his ma in shock. She refused to look at him. He could tell she felt vindicated that what she was doing was the right thing for the family.

Seeing his sister's familiar *I won* expression, he took a deep breath, turned, and left. He slammed the screen door behind him and walked back to the team of horses.

"What am I going to do?" Matthew cried to himself. "This isn't right!

"I did everything and more to keep this farm!

"This is how I am repaid!"

The depth of his grief and anguish was overwhelming. He twisted his hands around his handkerchief over and over as he walked back towards his team of horses. He had hoped his brothers would understand what the farm meant to him and his family. After all, they had heard the Leroy stories over and over throughout their lives.

Pa had emphasized that the most deserving son should inherit the farm. That's me. And he promised. We shook on it. I've done my part in honoring that promise. Pa failed to do his part, just like when his own father failed to disregard tradition and give the farm to him.

He knew none of that mattered to Maggie. She'd said she didn't believe her pa would make such a promise. That he loved all of them. He'd heard that there were times she took a loan from him for the store to pay vendors. Whether the loans were repaid or not, he didn't know. But there must have been a reason she'd been so determined to take away the farm.

Grace and he had talked about it but were fearful and were embarrassed by what Maggie was saying about them, making them sound like thieves. Neither knew what to do and were afraid of saying or doing anything to make it worse.

I fulfilled my pa's dream. I helped him create his legacy. He failed, just like his own pa.

Matthew sobbed as he turned the team around to the next row and set the spikes of the iron machine to move the dirt between the rows. He blindly followed the horses as they moved down the field.

Catherina – July 8, 1939

Catherina sat stunned after Maggie and Matthew left. Both her papa and uncle bequeathed their properties to her two brothers, but neither of them had wanted the old homesteads. Her only inheritance had been the coin-filled leather pouch Papa Henry had placed in her hands during their final goodbye.

Promises were not put in writing. A family's verbal promise needed to be honored.

"I don't know what to do to make this right," Catherina cried to herself.

It never occurred to her to talk with Adam or seek her own lawyer. Families didn't do that to one another. At least, good families did not. They worked it out among themselves quietly, hoping no one learned of their secrets. But that was now impossible.

Catherina thought back over the past hour and why Maggie had so much venom.

"Don't you want the Gunther name to be well thought of in honor of Pa?" Maggie had demanded.

Catherina had retorted with fire in her eyes, "Of course! How can you ask such a thing?"

"Then, you need to do what's right and sign the will. It gives each of us equal shares in the farm. We can each have our own parcel to do with as we want. That'd be what pa wanted … to ensure his legacy lived on."

Catherina sighed. *When Magdalena decreed the right thing to do, she expected everyone to follow along and not cause problems. Usually, they did since it was easier to go along to get along.*

"But what about your pa's promise …?" Catherina started to say but was cut short by Maggie yelling, "But Pa wouldn't do that to us! He loved us all. Matthew has been freeloading here for far too long. It's time he got his own place!"

Catherina shook her head while she stared down at her tightly clasped hands. *I don't know what to do. No one is listening to what George promised. There's just too much anger directed at Matthew with Magdalena's bitterness fueling the fire. He'll never be able to continue living here with so much animosity. Magdalena and her siblings would ensure their anger would be heard and felt for the rest of his life. They would have no qualms about shaming him for taking everything that they valued most.*

"It's a terrible day when a family is willing to sacrifice one another at one person's expense. It hasn't even been a month since I buried my husband and already all this …" Catherina exclaimed, standing up and looking up into Magdalena's eyes.

But Maggie was unwilling to back down.

"It'll be a better day once you do what is right," Magdalena stated.

Catherina stared back at her until Magdalena looked away. She looked down at her oldest daughter's fists clenching and unclenching and shook her head.

Catherina heard a voice out of nowhere. *You cannot win this alone, and Matthew doesn't have what it takes to fight them either.* She sat down defeated and stared at the paper that would forever change her family.

With shaky hands, she picked up the pen on the table and signed the will.

I just don't have the energy to fight all of them, Catherina said to herself later that afternoon when she was alone.

Catherina was angry for days to come at her daughter for splintering the family that George and she had nurtured for so many years. Family unity and a prosperous farm were their pride and legacy in life … George's dream. Now it was tarnished by Magdalena's pride … and that of her siblings.

Her greatest regret was failing at the time-honored tradition of honoring one's husband. George had made a promise to Matthew, a son who had toiled long hours in the heat of summer and the cold of winter to keep the farm. Because of him, they prospered.

The regret over what she had done was overwhelming. It never occurred to her, or anyone else, to direct her anger at George for not putting his promise in writing. Now, everyone was blaming her for this travesty.

Matthew – July 8, 1939

Dusk was settling with the stars blinking awake in the sky. It was time to drive the workhorses back to the barn for their nightly ritual.

Mathew's mind still churned between shock and disbelief. Anger had seeped into his heart and mind at his ma. It was her job to do what her husband said.

All these years of struggle, sacrifice, and hard work were for nothing.

I'm too old to start over. What'll I do? What'll I tell Grace and the girls? Grace didn't want to live and work here in the first place. She never trusted my siblings … and for good reason. Paulina has been calling them "shysters."

Every so often he reminded himself that fifty percent of these crops were his. He'd make sure he got every penny for them.

They'd need to move.

But where would they go?

It was dark when Matthew walked through the door of his home. His family looked at him and saw the grief etched on his weathered face.

Grace sighed and feared what he'd say. She hustled everyone to the table. After they had sat down to the family's favorite meal of fresh green beans, potatoes, ham, and cornbread, he told them what had happened. Each of them sat there speechless and unable to eat. They were stunned and scared at what this meant for them.

"Where will we live? What will happen to us?" Paulina expressed the fears that everyone was feeling.

Emma thought back to one of her cousin's comments in school that day: "Who do you think you are, trying to steal our farm?"

Now the comment made sense. But she didn't share the hurtful comments with her family. Their harassment was nothing new and would only add more upset to her dad's grief right now.

No one looked at each other. They stared at their food until Grace said, "Let's eat and not let the food get cold."

They picked up their forks and played with their food. The news was so horrible that finally Patti, the youngest daughter, started sobbing. She didn't fully understand what was happening, but knew it was bad.

Emma feared what would happen to them. She wasn't sure she could leave for college in the fall. It was a dream she had had since visiting her aunt Rachel and attending a University of Wisconsin travel program.

Susan was already living with Aunt Rachel. Someone would need to break the news to her. Emma doubted Susan would move back home to help since Susan hated living on the farm and the chores.

She didn't know if her aunt Rachel already knew and was part of this mess or not.

"I knew you couldn't trust that old battle-ax," Paulina finally broke the silence. She hissed, "The shysters!"

All of them were angry at how the Gunther family treated them for so many years. Usually, when Paulina complained to Grace about it, Grace would remind her, "Keep quiet about how you feel. We have to live here for a long time."

This time Grace nodded and didn't shush her.

Catherina and Matthew – July 8, 1939

They heard the light rap on the door. It stopped. Then, it sounded again. They froze since it was rare for them to have visitors at this time of the evening. They feared receiving more bad news.

Matthew stood up and hitched up his sagging pants. He opened the door to see his ma standing there.

It was rare for her to walk over to their home. Her German heritage dictated that a traditional sign of respect was for them to come to her, not for her to go to them.

Catherina glanced at Grace and each of her granddaughters and saw the tears. They know. She acknowledged them with a slight nod of her head and hoped they saw the sadness in her face.

Then, she turned to look at Matthew and commanded with a tilt of her head, "Come."

He walked outside and closed the door behind him.

Grace hurried over to crack open the door.

Emma ran as fast as she could upstairs to an open bedroom window so she could listen.

After Matthew and Catherina had walked to the edge of the cornfield, she thrust a fat old cowhide pouch in his hand. "Here, take this. It's yours. You've earned it," she said quietly.

She told him what her Papa Henry had whispered in his broken English so many years ago. "Keep this safe. Use it to prosper. Never forget your family is most important."

Matthew could tell by feeling the pouch that it contained coins and paper bills. He'd not seen it before and wondered where his ma had kept it hidden.

"Remember, you've worked hard for this. You're not to ever say anything about this. Ever. I'll deny it," Catherina stated emphatically.

Then, she added, "I went to the bank and had all the coins valued since they were given to me by my Papa Henry when we left Ohio back in 1866. But I kept four of them so you can give one to each of the girls. Someday they will be worth even more money than they are now."

Matthew looked down at the pouch. In the moonlight, he could see it was old and weathered, like he felt. He knew it was a payoff to not cause any trouble for the family. He didn't know yet what it would cost him to keep his silence.

Buying away her guilt was all he could think.

His dream was gone, stolen in a moment that could have been different had his ma stood up and told the truth to everyone. Or if his pa had put his promise in writing as he had said he would.

His relationship with his siblings was damaged beyond repair. All the years of ignoring the hurtful gossip and being called "thieves" and "freeloaders" had taken their toll. He could no longer pretend it didn't matter.

I'm too old and tired to build a new farm. An established farm is beyond anything I can afford. Plus, I don't have a son to help, or to inherit when I die, so, there is no use in starting over again.

Emma is ready to leave for college in two months. Susan is already gone. But I have two younger school-age daughters living at home.

It was too much change to grasp all at once, nor could he make any decisions now about what to do. But he had to protect his girls and wife first.

Catherina looked up at his sad face and down at his hands with dirt underneath his fingernails. She knew he'd honored his word. He'd done it with goodwill and had been easy to get along with, unlike his siblings always telling her and their pa what they should and shouldn't do with the farm.

Her heart didn't often go out to anyone. But at that moment, her heart grieved for him at depths unknown to her. She felt her own tears threaten to spill over and down her face. She resisted them. *Now is not the time.*

224 | The Old Wooden Rocker

Matthew – July 8, 1939

"Why, Ma?" Matthew asked. He had trouble getting those two words out. But like a lion suddenly under threat, he knew it was time to fight for what was his.

He repeated, "Why?"

"My Papa Henry told me to use them to prosper. I've added to them over the years," Catherina said quietly. Her tears were waiting to flow. "Now, I'm telling you the same."

They stood there for several minutes. They watched the fireflies twinkle off and on as they darted around the field of corn.

"Why?" Matthew asked a third time. He wasn't grasping the finality of it all.

"You know how Magdalena can be. You can't continue living here with your brothers all riled up and the community taking sides. They'll be angry at you and your family for the rest of your lives. I don't have the fight in me. I doubt you have the fight in you. We all need to get along with each other in order to live with one another. We are family. You and your siblings are all each other will have after I'm gone," Catherina said.

I don't know how to fix it. It had become the phrase she repeated to herself over and over.

Matthew's hands continued tightening and loosening his grip on the leather pouch.

When he could talk, there was a catch in his voice, "It's a little too late for that, Ma. I trusted you to honor Pa's promise."

A silence settled between them and lengthened as they both looked up at the full moon beaming down in all its glory on the green and growing foliage. It would be a very good crop, unless a storm damaged it.

Matthew then continued, "We'll be out of here as soon as we can. I will wait until the end of the harvest season. I want my money and don't trust my siblings to honor what is due me or the monies I've invested during these past years."

He felt the anger well up inside of him at the finality of it all.

"The money we paid so you could keep all of this." He swept his arm across the landscape.

"The money we invested in each year's crops." His hand dropped to his side and his shoulders drooped in defeat.

He lifted his head to look at her. "You will need to get another tenant farmer after the harvest to take care of the animals. I'm taking mine with me. We've got some new hogs that need to be sold before I leave."

Insistently, he added, "I'm taking the horses with me. They are mine. I paid for them with my labor."

Catherina said, "You should take all the animals since you did all the work to take care of them. We'll let Magdalena take care of the rest of it. Maybe she'll develop an understanding of your hard work. You and your family have done a lot during these past years. I thank you."

Matthew straightened his shoulders and said with more force than he intended, "I doubt it. I'll never get back my investment. The 50/50 split. The work done to remove stumps and clear land for more usable acreage. All to please Pa and you

226 | The Old Wooden Rocker

and create a legacy for me and my family to carry on. It was all done for nothing."

He swallowed hard to make sure he didn't unleash the anger that had turned into fury ... not yet. After all, she was still his ma.

He wanted to yell, *How dare you! It was mine!*

Instead, he said, with a hard edge to his voice, "It won't change anything."

His spirit was decimated. His pride forever tarnished. His birth family forever unforgiven.

It was unbelievable to work so hard for something and have it taken away so suddenly, so unfairly. He felt he was living in a nightmare.

There was silence, except for the crickets making their presence known, and the rustle of the corn leaves during a sudden breeze.

Catherina stood silent for a moment as she watched the shadows from the moonlight play over the corn crop. "No, it won't change anything. Land is property. It's a sign of prosperity. Your pa and I did well. You carried on his dream well. He was proud of you and what we'd accomplished."

Her words forever silenced any hope of waking up from this nightmare. His heart hardened.

She paused, then continued in a choked voice, "Your brothers have made money from working with their own farms. Your sisters are doing well. Sadly, I know they don't realize that owning more property won't make them any happier. But it gives them pride in this community to carry on the Gunther family name. It allows them to hold their heads high."

He replied angrily, "Yet you're rewarding them for not helping during these years. You're rewarding them for tearing apart our family."

He paused before adding, "At my expense."

Catherina replied in an even tone of voice, "They didn't help out on the farm like you did. That's true. They have their own farms. But as their ma, I know they helped in their own way. This farm prospered." Tears glistened in her eyes. She hoped her words found a soft place in his heart to hear what she was saying.

Matthew shook his head in disbelief at what he was hearing. *It's so wrong …*

He wasn't done yet. "Have you already forgotten? They weren't here day after day to endure the struggles of keeping this farm going. They weren't here when times were hard, to plow, till, and harvest the crops. Sitting up late into the night when animals were ill or having trouble birthing their next generation. My family had to trudge in the mud or snow up the hill to ensure you had milk and eggs every day. We fed the livestock daily, regardless of rain, wind, heat, and snow. In turn, we all were able to eat daily.

"This farm prospered during these past years due to my hard work … and that of my entire family. Now you're stealing it away from us. We've done nothing wrong." He was tired of repeating himself and listening to her excuses. No one was listening!

"Pa made me a promise to give me the farm when he died. You were there when we shook hands on it. Now you're taking away that promise. In doing so, my so-called brothers have been able to own farms because I did all the work here. My family, me and my wife and my daughters sacrificed and struggled to ensure you received fifty percent of everything."

Matthew continued, almost shouting, "We paid for fifty percent of everything! Now they will prosper off all my work. At my expense. What's in it for me? This is all about money and not letting someone else have more than they do. You. Know. It's. True." He spat out the last words.

Catherina looked at him with compassion. She wasn't surprised by his depth of anger. It was due.

She had already expressed her own anger at Magdalena for splintering the family further. She prayed her eldest daughter would live to regret her actions for the rest of her life.

Her distress of not honoring her husband's wishes made her angry. She had hoped and prayed for a way out of this nightmare. When George and she had listed the Gunther farm in her sole name on the deed, it was to avoid this splintering of the family. Now she could see it had been an ill-advised plan designed by George, fearful of the aftermath of writing and notarizing his promise to Matthew.

She said solemnly, "Everything you've said is true. Maybe in the future, you will come to understand our appreciation … your pa's and mine. You've done well and made us proud. I pray someday you and your children will understand the difficulty all this caused me. Remember, your brothers and sisters are my family, too."

Matthew stood there shaking his head in disbelief.

He said with bitterness in his voice, "Ma, you're mistaken. You're wrong … so … so wrong. I'm so glad I don't have any sons. They won't have to relive this illusion of family taking care of one another. They won't have to struggle like we did with family fighting among themselves!"

Exhausted from all the harshness he experienced this tragic day, he turned to walk away, then suddenly stopped.

"What would you have done if this had been in writing?" he asked.

Catherina paused before turning to walk up the hill to her old farmhouse. She said in a loud whisper, "We'll never know."

Then, she asked in a hopeful tone, "Did your pa put it in writing?" He shook his head back and forth with the moonlight reflecting off the top of his bare head.

He persisted, "I trusted both of you. Both of you gave your word to me. We shook hands on it. We were family!"

She again replied in a tearful whisper, "Then, we'll never know." The tears finally won as she turned and walked slowly back to the family home.

Without another word, he threw his arms into the air, silently cursing God. He was careful not to lose any of the precious gold coins or paper bills that held his family's salvation.

He turned and walked up to the tenant house where Grace stood in the doorway waiting and handed her the pouch without a word.

Then, he walked up the dark path following the flickering lights of the fireflies to the barn. His refuge was with his horses.

As he curried the horses, he shamelessly sobbed.

He was thankful Grace and the girls were resourceful. Together they would find a way. In anguish, he couldn't stop thinking, *I have nothing left to show for all my hard work.*

With a deeply broken heart, he felt like ending his life. A life that could never heal from this travesty. The horses stood, sensing something was very wrong. Their quietness interrupted with snorts and an occasional whinny or hoof stomp or tail swish, bringing comfort to his broken soul and a reminder that they needed him … just like his wife and daughters.

Matthew inhaled the scent from the horses while he worked over the next several hours. The repetitive motion soothed his heart.

Emma had overheard everything. In turn, she shared it with her mom and sisters. While they waited for their dad to return home, the younger two cried in fear of not knowing what would happen next. Susan went to hide in their bedroom.

Emma and Grace stoically sat and waited after they opened the pouch and counted out the cash. Then, they blew out a surprised whistle. It was over $900, plus four gold coins!

Finally, when the clock struck nine, Grace walked up the hill to the barn following the light from the fireflies. She found Matthew and gently asked, "Are you ready to come back home? We love you." She told him how much money was in the pouch and he looked at her in surprise.

He nodded and offered a small smile. The money didn't mend the hole in his heart, but it was more money than he'd ever had in his life.

She held out her hand and he grasped it as the lifeline it was. They walked back home without saying a word.

Through his tears, he noticed the fireflies had stopped blinking.

Jacob – July 10, 1939

Two days later, Jacob found Matthew working in the field. He had come over to talk with him after hearing from Maggie. She had grinned and waved the signed will in the air like a victory flag around noon the same day their ma had signed it.

He waited until Matthew stopped the horse team and turned his body to face him.

After they nodded at one another, Jacob asked, "Is there a reason you're not using the tractor?"

Matthew simply shrugged and waited. He was like his pa who didn't like change and wanted to save gas. And he enjoyed working with the horses.

Then, after several minutes of talking about the hot weather and this year's corn crop, Jacob finally got down to business.

"Why do you feel this family farm should be only yours?" Jacob asked, keeping his face neutral. He was trying not to sound accusatory like his sister had done.

"Because Pa promised it to me!" Matthew said with a hard edge in his voice and fury in his eyes. He mopped his brow with his handkerchief after removing his hat.

Jacob reeled from the intensity of Matthew's anger. It upset him to think their pa would give the entire farm to only one brother.

"Please. Tell me. What happened?" Jacob asked. It just didn't make sense that his pa would favor one son over the others. His deepest fear was afraid Maggie had driven the final spike splintering the family after Peter had been chiseling away at it for so many years. *I need to hear it in Matthew's own words.*

He hated change. He hated losing family and had been sad when his oldest son married and moved to Detroit to work on the auto line with Peter. Of course, he could never admit his own words and actions had been splintering family unity for many years.

Although he wanted to hear Matthew's version of events, the truth no longer mattered at this point. The ink had dried on the will. He prayed that Matthew wasn't going to fight it. There were six of them against one of him and they would do whatever it took to win. At least he hoped that was true. He hadn't spoken to anyone but Maggie. It wouldn't end well for Matthew and the Gunther name.

As the eldest son, he believed it was his job to resolve the matter. It never occurred to him he could have changed the outcome sooner. Gossiping, name-calling, and ignoring family harmony subtly created the inevitable outcome over many, many years. But he hadn't felt strong enough to weather the conflicting forces of both Maggie and Peter. Their never-ending anger at life was taken out on family members at different times. They were like locomotives bearing down without regard to anything in their way.

As his wife, Merry, had pointed out last night, it was too late to change anything. The damage had already been done and the hard feelings forever etched into his and Merry's hearts.

"Let this be a lesson for you after the way you talked about Matthew and his family!" Merry had said. "Without them, you wouldn't even have a family farm to divide. Now, what are you going to do about it?"

Before slamming the bedroom door in his face, she said, "Our family name is being tarnished again! You need to stop it! You're the oldest son. It's up to you!"

Jacob feared what the community and church would think of him and the Gunther family. Another brother forced out of the community. The farming community had come to recognize Matthew's hard work. They were impressed by his success both with farming and with training horses.

But they had also expressed concerns about Matthew's living off his parents' generosity for so many years, mostly due to the stories Peter had told and retold for so many years that others took as fact.

No one had known until yesterday when the gossip circulated faster than a wildfire that there had been a 50/50 arrangement. Not that it changed the outcome.

Jacob shook his head as thoughts swirled in his head while he waited for Matthew to respond. He could see his brother forming the words in his head.

Matthew spoke hesitantly. He was uncertain what to say since the truth no longer mattered. He wasn't afraid of his oldest brother. But his anger still simmered, and he felt the burden of blame for his pa's inability to do the right thing.

He told Jacob the whole story. He never considered lying. It was hard to share something that had consumed his life for so many years in a positive way and ended with such a devastating outcome.

Jacob stood there with his mouth gaping open, shaking his head in disbelief over the events that had occurred. They both had tears in their eyes. To hide their emotions from each other, they looked yonder or patted a horse. Jacob adjusted his flat cap to cover his eyes.

"I find it hard to believe that Pa made that promise," Jacob said. "Particularly, after all these years of listening to those stories about Leroy." He finally felt the upset pass.

"Yet I understand why Pa was desperate to keep this farm. His pride was at stake. Our family name painted in bold white letters on the old red barn. I'm so sorry it turned out this way."

Jacob patted the rump of the workhorse as he did his best to stay in control. It was a difficult conversation. It was worsened by the fact he felt helpless to change the outcome.

Now he knew the truth. Maggie had gotten it wrong. She had broken up the family to ensure Rachel and she got a share of the farm. He doubted the girls even needed the money! There had been no compassion or understanding for the truth. The reality was she was still exerting control and manipulating the outcome so as not to be humiliated by another "Maggie incident."

If only I'd known, we could have worked something out.

"Do you understand that there is nothing I can do now? I wish Pa had had the gumption, as he demanded of his own pa, to disregard tradition. But because he didn't, like his own pa didn't, there's nothing I can do," Jacob said.

If it had been me, I would be furious. More than Matthew, Jacob thought to himself. *But I would have also made the old man put it in writing.*

"You could tell the others the truth," Matthew said, emphasizing each word.

Jacob shook his head. "I will. But you know your brothers. Peter will call you a liar. Maggie will back his story. Benjamin's focus is on counting the days to jump on the train out of here. Everyone has had their eyes on owning or selling this property since we were old enough to want it. Maggie fueled the flames. I trust the fire will die down in time. But Adam filed the will yesterday. It's done."

Matthew slumped in despair. There had been a very small glimmer of hope when he saw Jacob arrive. Now hopelessness invaded his entire body.

He glared at his oldest brother. "Why are you here then? To gloat?"

Jacob looked genuinely hurt. "No. Of course not!" he said, tipping his cap back on his head. He felt more confident in this part of the conversation.

"I came to be sure I learned the true story. Not that it'll make a difference for what you'll need to do," Jacob replied calmly.

Matthew shook his head with an uncharacteristic scowl on his face. His fate was sealed.

They stood there, eyeing the red wheat and oats that would soon be harvested. As they stood uncomfortably toeing the dirt with their work boots, neither knew what else to say.

Then Jacob had an idea.

"I'll tell you what I can do," he said with sudden conviction as he twirled his cap from hand to hand in nervousness.

"I know it won't make the situation any better. I talked with ma earlier to hear her side of it. She's very upset over all this. I've never ever seen her cry before, even when we buried Pa. I know I can't make it right in your eyes, or in hers. But I'll let you have the first pick of the parcel of acreage," Jacob offered.

"How will you do that? Ma should have told the truth from the beginning. Then none of this would have happened," Matthew replied with anger. He stood gazing defiantly at the woods lining the back forty acres.

"There's nothing else I can do. While your version and Ma's are the same, Maggie will challenge it and make you both look like liars. As you've seen, Maggie can be like a cornered animal. She'll make a vicious attempt to get and defend what she believes is only right." Jacob paused.

"Think back to when Nathan left. She was so embarrassed and fearful of what others would think. She sued him for the house and store during the divorce to prove he was a bad man for leaving Nathaniel and her. Though to this day, no one knows what happened ... or they aren't talking."

Then, he added in a quiet, yet firm, voice, "Legal action would make the situation even worse for the family. You wouldn't want the burden of that on your shoulders, would you?"

One of the horses swished its tail into Jacob's face and knocked the cap off his head. He bent down to pick it up while moving farther away from the horse's hoof. He stalled for time by deliberately brushing the dirt off his cap before putting it back on his head. The second time he caught the horse's tail before it hit him in the face. He moved still farther away from the back end of the horse.

Matthew pressed his lips together while looking down at his feet. It was to hide his grin. Alas, Jacob did not have a sense of humor. He failed to have sympathy for others, especially those who struggled to make ends meet.

While Matthew was not book smart like his two oldest daughters, Susan and Emma, he could read people. He felt disgusted at Jacob's poor attempt to offer an olive branch, as though that would make everything all right. Matthew could also tell Jacob was uneasy and nervous having this conversation but felt no compassion for him.

He's only trying not to feel guilty. Matthew thought, while his anger subsided. *It's over; it's done. There's nothing more to do except get my money from the crop sale and sell any of the animals I don't want to take with me.*

He remembered that when he was young, there were many times Jacob, Peter, and Maggie would have shouting matches to see who was the loudest. He and his younger brothers and sister watched with fear etched on their young faces until both their parents shushed and threatened them!

While Maggie was the domineering one and often won, Jacob would simply do what was expected regardless of what was right. Peter was the hothead who used his anger to cover up his laziness. It was why they dubbed him Leroy.

They stood there several minutes not looking at each other. Then, Jacob broke the silent impasse. He said, "Maggie believes she should have whatever she wants first because she's the oldest. Instead, I'll insist you choose which parcel you want first. Ma will back me up. Remember, the deed is still in her name."

"It won't right the wrong!" Matthew said. He felt so alone. His birth family would not fight for him and do the right thing … but then they never had … calling him and his family names and failing to offer to help over the years. He felt powerless to do anything different.

Matthew didn't trust his eldest brother. They had never been close. Jacob's sons had been calling Matthew's daughters liars and thieves since his family had moved into the tenant house back in 1927.

Even though Jacob and Peter were the only ones who could stand up to Maggie, it was debatable if either could win. Peter would have no interest in doing so with dollar signs in his eyes. Jacob would either honor his word or fail like his pa had already done.

"The truth is, we would have fought you. But I'll tell your side of the story. Our brothers are afraid to ask you themselves. They fear Maggie and the repercussions of not agreeing with her. I'll let them know you deserve to have first pick," Jacob said. "I know this is of little consolation but it's the best I can do."

There was nothing more for the brothers to say to one another. It was their last conversation.

But Jacob hated the uncomfortableness and attempted to ease the conversation to a close. "I'll tell our brothers the truth; yet, as you know, I can't change what others in our community will say. You know they can be worse gossipers than women."

Matthew did not smile.

There was a long pause as the horses whinnied and started stomping to get rid of the flies. Then, Jacob hurriedly continued, "My point is I can't control what they think or say."

Matthew said nothing as he picked up the reins for the team of horses.

"What do you plan on doing?" Jacob asked in his last attempt to hold on to his brother for a few minutes longer.

He spoke fast before Matthew could respond. "Ma has agreed we can split up the property now. A pre-estate event. Everyone will get their parcel to farm or sell it. She will sign quit claim deeds. Depending on what happens, I promised her I would include in my parcel the old farmhouse so she can continue living there until her death. Her *old farmhouse*, as she calls it."

When Jacob finally stopped, they both were silent until Matthew offered, "We'll get another place." It was all that he would say. Then, he added in a whisper, "Far away from here."

"Let me know how we can help. You are my brother, and I do care," Jacob said as he gave a final pat to the horse's rump.

Matthew shouted, "Gee" and the impatient horses moved. They had stood too long in the hot sun. As they moved away from Jacob, Matthew wanted to lash out and say, "If you care so much, make this go away. It's my farm. I'm the one that did all the work all these years."

"God be with you," Jacob called after him.

He was emotionally exhausted. He knew he would never see Jacob or his siblings again after harvest. "They betrayed me and my family. It's unforgivable they would do that to me.

This illusion of a family working together for the good of the family name. Pfft," he whispered out loud.

He felt his manhood and pride had been knocked down to nothing.

At that moment, he decided to hold his head high. *I cannot trust asking anyone for help. My good name and honesty have been diminished in the eyes of the very people I've grown up with. The same ones I gave a helping hand to and whose horses I trained. It's a sin that the great Gunther & Sons family farm is a legacy now tarnished by greed.*

Catherina – September 1939

Jacob kept his word to Matthew.

Catherina supported it and dictated that Matthew get the first pick after a professional survey was completed.

Maggie was angry and screamed, "No, he won't! The oldest should go first!"

"I'm still alive. It's my property. I. Will. Do. It. My. Way. Or I'll get my own lawyer and have the will rewritten," Catherina shouted. Her shock had finally evolved into righteous anger over what her children had forced her to do to Matthew.

Maggie backed off as fast as she could. She remembered what Adam had told her about not forcing or intimidating their ma. While her ma was not a revengeful person, she still feared Adam having the sheriff arrest her and never being able to hold her head high again.

Matthew picked the prime acreage after the professional survey. Then Rachel and he sold their parcels for more than the going rate for farmland. He found out later she would have supported him but reminded him a legal fight would have only made things worse.

Many of the other parcels were sold during the following years. Jacob and Charlie kept and farmed theirs. Then, they bequeathed their land in writing with equal shares given to their sons and Charlie included his one daughter. A new tradition had begun.

But the old legacy refused to go away and waited patiently to pounce again.

November 1939

It was a crisp autumn day when Matthew and his family left. The leaves had already turned brilliant reds, oranges, and yellows. The grasses were dull brown. The harvest was completed, animals except for the horses sold, and the money divided between Matthew and his ma.

There was no get-together to wish Matthew and his family farewell. They had stopped attending church and other community events back in the summer when all this controversy could no longer be kept a family-only matter. They didn't even attend or enter the county fair. In the past, the family often won money and blue ribbons.

Emma left for college in the fall to take advantage of her scholarship at the University of Wisconsin after her parents urged her to do so. They knew Rachel would help her through this difficult time, just as she was already helping Susan cope with the betrayal.

The day before the family left to travel to their new home, which was an hour away by horse and wagon, Catherina gave them many pieces of the furniture George had made over the years. She wanted them to have something for their new home.

The day the caravan of autos and trailers (driven by Grace's two brothers and sister) followed the team of horses drawing the wagon with all their belongings, she had stood alone and erect on her front porch watching them disappear down the dirt road. Her hand shaded her eyes against the glare of the morning sun. No one waved or said goodbye. There were no hugs. All eyes were kept averted from her.

Her heart had broken into pieces that would never heal together again.

Without moving, she stood there long after the dust settled. It was one of few times in her life, although much more often as of the past few months, she allowed the tears to roll down her wrinkled and weathered face. She didn't swipe at them in denial that they existed.

This was her greatest regret.

While Matthew and Emma visited Catherina once a year out of a sense of obligation, Grace and her other daughters refused to do so. They were not invited to any Gunther family holiday festivities, weddings, or graduations. None of Matthew's family attended Maggie's or Catherina's funerals.

Everyone's pride prevented them from offering an olive branch of forgiveness, fearing they would be swatted with it. Time did not heal the pain of familial betrayal.

PART 8

Forgiveness is a process of letting go.
If you wait too long, it can often be too late.

Rachel – 1944 to 1950

After Emma graduated from the University of Wisconsin, Rachel spoke with pride about her niece's accomplishments. Emma was the first woman in the family to graduate from college with not just one degree, but two! She had earned both bachelor's and master's degrees in education. She had accepted a teaching position in Milwaukee and Rachel and Susan helped her move.

A few weeks later, Rachel received a missive from Maggie telling her to stop talking about their nieces' successes. In future letters, Rachel stopped sharing the news with her family since it only seemed to cause controversy.

Rachel gave Emma money as a graduation gift. In turn, Emma purchased her own property next to her parents' new farm and rented it out to the same farmer her parents rented their land to.

Rachel had laughed and clapped her hands with glee when Emma told her what she had done. Rachel called her "my budding property owner." She prayed Emma's sisters would see the wisdom of investing their money too. But the youngest two were more interested in spending it and finding husbands … as long as the young men were not farmers!

Times are changing for women … but not fast enough, Rachel thought as she sat by her bay window and watched the street activity below. *Life and society still treated them as second-class citizens, especially young single women. My prayers for Susan and Emma include faring well alone since there don't appear to be any marriage prospects for either of them. I also pray for their two younger sisters. It was good to see them moving on after the break-up of the family.* She set her devotional guide on the table next to her recliner.

Rachel was surprised that her ma hadn't been impressed by Emma's hard work.

"Why she needs to do that, I'll never understand. Women are not meant to work men's jobs," Catherina complained. Rachel smiled at her.

"Today's teachers need college degrees to teach in the city schools," She replied.

"Hmph. They don't need it to get married and be good wives."

Rachel replied, "Not everyone needs to get married today. And, because of the war, there is a shortage of good men to marry!"

A week after the visit, Rachel received another written diatribe from Maggie. This one informed her that she was not helping the Gunther family with her lofty ideas about women working in men's jobs. Clearly, Catherina was sharing Rachel's conversations with Maggie.

"It would be in everyone's best interest if you encouraged Matthew's daughters to improve their behavior, so they are marriageable. Their father's greed … as you know … the apple doesn't fall far from the tree," Maggie wrote.

Yet she bragged about her son, Nathaniel, having received his degree in accounting. He'd been working in a big accounting company in Chicago and was being transferred to manage the LA office. She looked forward to seeing them as they traveled through Harrison on their way to Los Angeles.

"We are the black sheep of the family," Rachel whispered out loud with a grin on her face. "The strong women that help support strong men."

Albert used to call her with love and admiration, "my little black sheep," anytime she'd talk about her family's traditional points-of-view. It was his way of reminding her she couldn't change others' opinions … especially that fast. It took time, and many times it didn't happen until generations later.

Each night Rachel prayed for her family's understanding and acceptance of each other.

Every year out of a commitment to stay connected with her siblings, she visited her family in Harrison. She endured Maggie's rants about her selfishness and listened to Catherina's litany of concerns about it being unsafe for single women to live alone and travel by themselves. She never confided about her own travels out of fear they would fuel more controversy over how she chose to live her life.

As the years rolled by, even her brothers and their families made it clear they expected her to do the right thing and move back home. Mostly, they wanted her to live with their ma and take care of her so they didn't need to do so.

Her only ally was her sister-in-law, Melinda, Charlie's wife. Melinda encouraged her to live her life from her heart. Melinda's older sister had left home to live and work in a larger town. She'd been proud of her sister's accomplishments and ability to make a better life for herself as a professional woman. She hoped her daughter, Jessica, would have the courage to do the same. Rachel wished her siblings felt the same way about her.

In 1948, after a short visit from Matthew's youngest daughter Patti, Rachel sold her apartment in Madison and bought a small home in Albuquerque. Her niece, Susan, had already moved there after tiring of the snow and cold in Madison. It was where Grace's sister, Leticia, and her husband lived.

Before Rachel left Harrison, she had Adam draw up a new will for her, which bequeathed her money to charities for women, and equal amounts to each of Matthew's four daughters. She also left a small stipend to Jessica, her only other niece, even though she was concerned about the controversy it would cause the young woman since they didn't have a close relationship. But knew Melinda would handle any questions.

Over the years, she made an annual visit to Harrison to see her ma, Jacob, Charlie, and Maggie and their families living close by. Also, she continued to send gifts to Matthew and Grace, and to their daughters and families. That was her way of softening the horrendous situation and gossip that still circulated for far too many years. Maggie's need to wrest control away from all of them had left the siblings leery of working together and fearful of what she might do to them … even years later.

During the last few years of Catherina's life, she and her ma started to enjoy each other's company. It began with Catherina's comment, "I'm sorry I was so hard on you all these years. I just didn't want you to suffer. I wished I could have followed my own dreams of being a farmer."

Rachel was shocked by her ma's statement. Catherina had never apologized before and never shared about her dreams before marrying pa. Everything had been focused on her husband and his life and dreams like many women.

As her ma told her the story, Rachel sat in awe listening to her. She'd been so focused on her own life she forgot her ma had had her own life before her. It hadn't occurred to her that her ma's dreams differed from her pa's. Like her siblings, she assumed her pa's dream for the Gunther legacy was also hers.

Rachel responded with pride and a grin, "But you have become a farmer … a large landowner … largest in the county! Now, you've shared it with your children. You've been a strong and courageous influence as a woman. It's allowed each of us to pursue a life that was meaningful to us."

Catherina listened and didn't respond. But Rachel could tell she'd heard and felt the acknowledgment since there were tears running down her face.

Maggie – 1945

Maggie had been jubilant over her win of the Gunther estate and making her ma to do the right thing. She justified her actions by making sure Rachel and she got their shares along with each of her brothers. But in her zeal to win, she failed to consider honoring her pa's promise. It never occurred to her to work out a compromise that would have honored the Gunther legacy. Instead, Maggie allowed her anger at Matthew and her need to dominate the outcome to blind her to other options and tarnish the family name.

Now, she blamed Matthew for the family strife and secretly hoped he suffered for his greed.

Maggie had written Rachel about the will and Matthew's attempted theft after it happened. She imagined that Rachel would see the wisdom of what she had done and applaud her actions because they were now included in the division of the farmland. But she was very much mistaken.

The letter she received back from Rachel in 1939 expressed her upset:

> It breaks my heart that the closeness you and Matthew shared as children has been forever damaged again by your harsh words and harsher actions.
>
> I don't know what happened at the time of your high school graduation, since I was young. But I've been told by Ma that you became angry at Matthew at that time and never forgave him. She didn't know why. All I remember are the kittens in the barn and

Pa being angrier than I'd ever seen him before or after.

Regardless of what happened, I believe it is a travesty that Pa's promise to our brother was broken. If I had known what you were doing and had heard from Matthew, I would have done my best to put a stop to this unforgiving way of treating our brother.

While I understand that our brothers and you were unwilling to receive nothing, I was mortified that you ignored Pa's promise and coerced Ma into signing a will she didn't want to sign. I've checked; there is no law dictating that a father and mother must equally bequeath their children anything.

You've treated Matthew as the wrongdoer, instead of applauding all he'd done to keep the Gunther farm for Pa and Ma, especially during years of a great economic crisis.

Your thoughtlessness has cost us our brother. It would have supported Pa's and Ma's legacy, their dream, of having the outcome be handled in a loving and honorable way. They trusted their children to honor them and we have failed.

Your righteousness and your need to control everyone have hurt you. You may not recognize the impact of it for a long time to come. I pray someday you will be able to correct the horrendous wrong you've caused and ask for forgiveness.

Your sister, Rachel

Maggie had been furious and immediately ripped the letter in half and thrown it in the fireplace. *How dare she say that about me! She doesn't understand the sacrifices I made to protect our pa's legacy.*

In the years that followed, Maggie had had time to calm down. But her feeling of moral correctness never wavered. She thought, *If what I did was so wrong, Ma could have gotten an attorney, but didn't. Even after Jacob told Matthew it would be his fault if the Gunther family name was tarnished in a court trial, Matthew could have gotten an attorney too, but didn't. Rachel could have stepped up and hired an attorney while making her thoughts known but didn't.*

I wanted Pa's legacy to live on. I did what I had to do to make sure it happened the only way that was right! They should thank me!

But no one did. Over the years they came to blame Maggie for what had happened to Matthew. No one took responsibility for their own words and actions, or lack thereof.

Maggie refused to believe that Matthew and his family were the victims. She told anyone who asked about Catherina, "She bequeathed each of us the family farm now instead of waiting until after she passed. It was a generous gift to each of us."

Everyone in Harrison and surrounding farming communities heard the rumors. They'd say their prayers on Sundays and deny it could ever happen to them. After all, they believed they were good church-going people, so nothing like that would ever befall them. Maybe if the Gunthers had attended church more often …

And on it went.

Even though Matthew left the community with his head held high, some echoed Paulina's words, "the shysters." Some said that about Matthew, while others quietly renounced the false pride of all of them.

As the years went by, Maggie's anger towards Matthew never subsided. It simmered on top of the anger she still felt toward her former husband and being treated as a second-class citizen by townspeople. Even her son, Nathaniel called her a liar and blamed her for his father leaving him decades ago. He'd told her, "It's your fault for being so outspoken and domineering! You're a woman and need to know your place in life! It's embarrassing!"

According to Nathaniel, his father never contradicted him when Nathaniel shared his beliefs about why his father had left Harrison so many years ago.

Over time, Nathaniel and his mother became further estranged. They stopped speaking and writing to one another. Forgiveness wasn't possible.

Her solace was the substantial amount of money she received from selling her store and her Gunther & Son's parcel, which demonstrated she'd been right about so many things. She'd done it herself without any help from anyone else.

With a lot of time on her hands, she focused on playing cards with neighbors and attending community and church events to keep busy. She generously gave money to different causes in Harrison. Rachel had suggested she get involved in helping other women who were less fortunate. Maggie grudgingly did so, but over time, she found enjoyment in helping other women less fortunate than herself, especially when they looked up to her and thanked her for guiding their way.

Eventually, her brothers' families stopped inviting her to their homes. They didn't feel comfortable going to her home due to her exacting expectations of how to act, dress, and talk. Her sisters-in-law didn't kibbitz with her or stop by to talk with her after she sold the general store. Rachel would still make her annual visits, but never opened up about her life or invited her to come stay in her home.

Each family member believed their righteous silence was justified and felt Matthew's greed had gotten in his way of remaining part of the family. They'd done their best to forgive but believed praying for Matthew's sins guaranteed them a place in heaven. It never occurred to them that they could have prevented the damaging family legacy from being repeated.

Peter, Jacob, and Charlie – 1939 to 1945

When Jacob had told Peter Matthew's story in 1939, Peter called Matthew a liar and a thief.

He declared, "There's more to that story. I don't believe it. Benjamin doesn't either."

When Jacob talked with Benjamin, he shook his head at all the controversy and refused to join the fray. Instead, he focused on finalizing all his personal and farm matters before his long-awaited journey, though he did make sure Adam wrote a tight will in case someone got greedy, the lesson he learned from the family dispute.

Charlie and Jacob believed Matthew, but they were unwilling to do more than give Matthew the first option to select his parcel from the Gunther & Sons farm.

Peter hung onto his parcel and rented it out to a local farmer while he was working the second shift at an auto plant in Michigan. In 1945, when it was time to retire, Peter sold his parcel, but received less money than the others, as the market value had dropped.

He rationalized the lower sale price was due to the poor choice of land he had to pick from. As the second-oldest son, he believed he should have been able to pick the better parcels before his younger siblings and sisters. But he knew better than to share that opinion out loud. When he told family members Matthew had gypped him again, they stopped listening. Time had moved on.

Over the years, the oldest and youngest brothers focused on building their farms with the additional acreage. Jacob and Charlie believed their success and pride were testaments to God's benevolence for their hard work.

"Matthew's fall from grace must have been his own fault for thinking he could steal the Gunther & Sons farm from all of us," Peter said to Charlie.

Charlie shook his head but kept his thoughts to himself. He didn't want to irk Peter and have him turn his anger on him. After all, what was done was done.

But Charlie wasn't as forgiving as he pretended to be. He had a difficult time reconciling what Matthew had done. They had had a special brotherly bond as the youngest sons of George and Catherina, born less than 12 months apart.

His confusion about what was righteous in the eyes of God kept him away from Matthew and he never spoke to him again. He vacillated between judging Matthew as good or as greedy.

Before his pa died, Charlie stood up for Matthew when the townspeople made unkind comments. Charlie would reply, "My brother is a hard worker. His wife and daughters work hard too. Because my pa's an invalid, my brother's hard work allows my parents to keep their farm."

But now after the "Matthew incident," everything changed. He stopped saying anything about his brother.

Melinda and he discussed the situation at length over the years. Their feelings changed back and forth like the weather about what was right and what was wrong.

On one hand, they felt that Matthew working with their ma kept her from demanding too much from the rest of them. But on the other hand, and, depending on the value of their crops each year, they believed Matthew had conned their ma into promising him the farm or that, just possibly, their pa had made such a promise.

These never-ending thoughts and muddled feelings swayed Charlie's thinking about Matthew over the years. He allowed this confusion, rather than his brotherly love, to consume him for the rest of his life.

Like his older brothers, Charlie could not blame their beloved pa for what had occurred. It would be a sin to do so. After all, as the Bible stated, "Every one of you shall revere his mother and his father …"

They ignored the part about revering their ma, and quietly blamed her for the family splintering apart.

Catherina – May 5, 1950

In her dreams, Catherina kept reliving the memory of Matthew staring at her with sorrow. It broke her heart and saddened her soul.

After she awoke from her nap and calmed down from the sadness of the recurring dream, she spent thirty minutes looking through the pictures in her Bible. Even though she had seen them hundreds of times, they reminded her of much happier times.

Exhausted from the eye strain reading caused, she slowly turned to the page listing all the births and deaths in her family and laid her hands on the page in prayer. Then, with care, she closed and placed the old family Bible back on top of the checkerboard table. It was the *Holman's Edition, The Holy Bible* they had received when they were married. Over the years reading Bible passages aloud to George had brought them both peace.

Catherina's eyes fell on the tall wooden footstool with iron scrolling on each foot, another hand-made gift from George so she could sit and play. It stood in front of the upright wooden oak piano that was still in very good condition after all these years. It needed dusting … and probably needing tuning too since it hadn't been played in many years.

George had bought the turn-of-the-century family heirloom it when one of the gold-seekers needed money to get to California.

While she'd hoped Nathaniel would want the piano since he had a gift of playing by ear, he had told her to give it to someone else when he stopped by with his family on their way to LA.

George and she had loved listening to the music played by their children and grandchildren.

Rachel loved to sing and had the best voice. She sang in the church choir, while she did her chores around the house, and in the barn when it was her turn to milk the cows or clean stalls. But she refused to play and sing when visiting home after moving to Madison.

Even with all the changes in women's rights over the years, Catherina still had strong opinions that girls needed to live near their families until they married. Otherwise, these girls would be lonely and gain dubious reputations as old spinsters.

She had spent years praying for Rachel. Her youngest daughter's way of life had been her third most important regret. She believed she had failed her in some way when Rachel left home. It was difficult for her to understand why she'd felt the need to leave and live on her own in a big city. Who was going to take care of her in her older years? That's why you got married and had children … a lesson she had learned over the years.

Catherina still hoped for the miracle of Benjamin walking through the front door with that endearing lopsided grin, saying, "Hey, Ma. What's for dinner?"

Benjamin's disappearance was the second saddest regret in Catherina's life. She cherished the memories of her third son's easygoing nature. It was hard to know whether to grieve over his death or rejoice that he had been able to fulfill his spirit of adventure.

Not knowing what had happened to him tormented her. When Adam declared him dead, he'd given her the remaining money in Benjamin's bank account, but she told Adam to send it to Matthew.

Catherina slowly rocked as the light turned into darkness and the clock struck six. She felt around her to see if Blackie was still beside her, and gratefully petted him. He responded by rubbing his wet nose on the back of her hand.

There were no more tears to shed right now.

Is this all there is to life? You live, you die?

You work hard. You sweat and toil to keep your family together to survive and create a legacy for future generations. You hope that you are successful and pray that God is benevolent.

You survive all that life throws at you and pray God will not forsake you.

In the meantime, if you are fortunate, your children leave home to have their own children, and create their own legacies, and the cycle starts all over again.

If you're fortunate to live a long life and experience all of this, you look back at your memories and pray they will comfort you. You pray that you won't become a burden your family resents. When it's time to leave this earth, you pray your family learned from your mistakes and are not angry with you and fighting over your money and property.

This was the illusion of family unity, a sham and a curse, because families treated each other far worse than other people.

Maggie – May 11, 1950

It was mid-afternoon and the thunderstorm that had moved through earlier was gone. The electricity was back on, allowing Maggie to look through the mail in her small home office. The room was comfortable and lined with books and colored glass objects to make it restful and joyful. The thick drapes kept out the hot morning sun in the summer and the cold wind in the winter. The wooden desk was old and made of walnut. She'd had it refinished. Her chair was a padded Victorian that she'd bid on at an estate auction many years ago.

She spied a hand-written envelope from Adam. They had finalized her own will a month ago, and briefly talked about not knowing what had caused her divorce from Nathan.

She opened the envelope with her gold-plated letter opener and pulled out a hand-written notecard.

> *Dear Maggie,*
>
> *I'm so sorry. After our last conversation, I found out that you were being blamed for Nathan and his father leaving Harrison. I was meeting with the sheriff's wife, Sue Ellen, and she mentioned it unexpectedly.*
>
> *As you know, I moved back to Harrison from Madison to take care of my father's affairs when he passed in 1937 and I stayed.*
>
> *But I was there the night of the poker game, back in 1916, as were several others: Nathan,*

*his father, Benjamin, and the sheriff. We played
for money and were drinking shots of whiskey.
This was before Prohibition became the law of
the land. When I ran out of money, I left to
catch the last train back to Chicago/Madison
that evening. It was a Saturday night.*

*Sue Ellen mentioned that, after I had left the
poker game, there was a violent scuffle in the
back of the parsonage and someone may have
died. She wasn't sure since her husband didn't
tell her the details. She couldn't remember who it
was or why. But because of the serious injury
and possible death, your former husband and
his father left quickly to avoid being charged for
the crime. Your brother was sworn to silence.
Sue Ellen didn't know if it had been an accident
or not … or even if there had been a death since
there was never a notice in the paper to claim
the body.*

*This is all I know. You may wish to talk with
the sheriff's wife. Please accept my deepest
apology for not saying something sooner to ease
your sorrow.*

Sincerely, Adam

Maggie felt the heavy wall she'd built around her heart
crumble. It had safeguarded her grief and fury from feeling
blamed and abandoned by Nathan and his father, her pain

over Nathaniel's false accusations that she had caused his father to run away, the gossip and shunning she endured as a divorced woman, and now, her mother's and siblings' attacks for her work to fulfill her pa's wishes.

Long-forbidden tears flowed endlessly like a dam of water that could no longer be contained. She rarely allowed herself the luxury of feeling so deeply since it never felt safe to do so without someone using it against her.

But Adam's note was so kind. The vindication was so long overdue. The relief so, so comforting.

Finally, the truth. She continued sobbing and called out loud in anguish, "Why me?"

She'd had no one to confide in over the years. Her pa had withheld the truth. She refused to talk with Catherina, who couldn't understand. With no real close friends and not trusting Rachel to sympathize, she'd felt very much alone in life.

After patting her eyes, she looked down to see that her tears had washed out most of the handwritten note from Adam. She carefully placed the notecard back in its envelope and held it to her heart in appreciation before sliding it into the center desk drawer. After she locked the drawer, she went into the kitchen to find a cold compress for her eyes, feeling lighter than she had for most of her life.

Later that night she experienced chest pains from the weight of the anger and resentment that had been carried in her heart for far too long. Before she could reach for the phone and summon a neighbor to help her, her soul left peacefully to be reunited with her pa in heaven.

Nathaniel – May 16, 1950

Nathaniel wasn't surprised that Maggie's ma and her brothers and their families that lived in the Harrison area attended her funeral. But he was astonished by the number of townspeople attending too.

He plastered a sad, half-smile on his face while greeting everyone. But he wasn't grieving. He was surprised by the mourners consoling him and telling him about his mother's contributions to the town and church.

He nodded and said all the right words. But underneath his facade, he still blamed his mother for the Gunther family controversy and his father's living in exile.

After he'd buried her six feet in the grave between her pa and the headstone for his uncle Benjamin, he noticed there was an empty space for Catherina's death date underneath his grandpa's on his headstone. He'd be sad when he lost her after all the love she'd given him.

Nathanial attended the community dinner in his mother's honor.

The next day, he went to take one last look over any personal items of his mother's that he might want. He was aware that her will gave the old Victorian house where he'd grown up to a women's charity. But he was allowed to take whatever he wanted first before they took over.

His final act was cleaning out her desk. He'd leave the desk and books there for the charity to do with as they wanted. He looked at the colorful glass objects and shook his head at the wasted money since the items weren't cheap. *I'm surprised she didn't die in debt.*

He was almost done when he found the note from Adam. It started with, "I'm sorry ..." but the rest looked like his mother had spilled water on it. He sat shaking his head in annoyance. *Now what? I don't have time for all this.*

Before I leave, I better talk with Adam to make sure everything is done. I'm never coming back here, Nathaniel thought.

That afternoon Nathaniel met with Adam to tell him he was done and to give him the keys to the house.

Adam nodded before saying, "You know she left all her money and her pride, her Victorian home, to a charity where single women can live with their children. These women could be abused or widowed and without any money. She wanted to help them to get on their feet and live a better life. She owned her home free and clear. Rachel is named as chair of the board and responsible for disbursing funds. I'm also on the board to handle any legal concerns."

"What about the store?" Nathaniel asked matter-of-factly. Adam and he had already talked about the contents of the will. He wanted to review everything one last time so that there were no surprises or anything overlooked.

"That was sold back in 1945. She didn't owe any mortgage on it and paid off her home from the proceeds." Adam stated. "She was a wise businesswoman and money manager."

Nathaniel kept a serious face instead of saying, "I'm surprised."

They sat in silence for several minutes. Nathaniel finally asked Adam about the note he found.

"The ink was water-stained so I couldn't make it out. What were you sorry about?" Nathaniel. He handed Adam the note he'd found.

Adam's answer surprised him.

He began, "Your mother knew nothing about what happened so many years ago with your father. She never knew why Nathan had to leave town with your grandfather Landes. I was there the night it happened. We were playing poker. When I ran out of money, the amount I was willing to play, I left to catch the train back to Chicago."

Nathaniel nodded with an impatient look etched on his face, pretending to understand, but surprised his mother knew nothing about what had happened.

Adam continued, "You need to hear the whole story. Your mother knew nothing about the poker game. It was played at the parsonage with your father, grandfather Landes, Benjamin, the sheriff, and me. There were many shots of whiskey and money lost … this was before Prohibition. Just as I was leaving, a lady arrived that I'd not seen before. But I scurried out fast because I heard the train whistle announcing it would be in Harrison soon. I couldn't miss being on *that* train."

"Then, you don't know what really happened," Nathaniel stated with irritation creeping into his voice.

"Well … all I know was your grandpa Gunther was involved in getting your uncle Benjamin out of jail. Benjamin did tell me that much on one of his visits to Madison. And, that Nathan and his father left town immediately. The rest would be a story I made up," Adam said truthfully.

"I still don't understand what you're sorry about." Nathaniel insisted.

"When your mother came to have her will updated to leave everything to the women's charity, she mentioned that evening. She asked if I'd heard anything over the years. I said I had not. But later that evening I remembered the poker game, whiskey, and money. Then, by happenstance, I talked with the sheriff's widow the following day and she filled me in.

"You know your grandpa Landes was a wealthy man. He bought your father the general store that later become Maggie's from the divorce. Also, the house south on Main. But she sold that when she bought the Victorian house you grew up in. She lived there until she passed."

Adam inhaled and paused before speaking ill of Nathan. He continued, "Your father wasn't a man of character. He let your mother do most of the work in the store and lived off his father's money. Your mother pursued your father, seeing him as her way of getting off the farm. But your father wasn't a faithful man. He played around. It took a long time before the townspeople accepted her as one of their own."

"I still don't understand what you're sorry about." Nathaniel pointedly looked at his watch.

"She was falsely blamed for what happened that night. She wasn't there. I left early so I don't know all the details. I didn't discuss it in full with Benjamin since he was reluctant to tell all that had happened … something about your grandpa George's adamant desire to keep the whole situation silent. As you know, the sheriff died back in the '30s."

Nathaniel let out a huge sigh and asked with annoyance, "Okay. And?"

"I felt badly that she was blamed and I didn't even know about it. If I had known, I would have said something sooner. She didn't even know who had been there, what had happened, or why her husband and father-in-law disappeared so fast without a word to her."

"Okay. But it doesn't excuse her getting a divorce or explain why she was always angry."

"Well, the divorce was handled by an attorney who is no longer living. I understand your grandpa Gunther was involved and he is gone too. Adam said. "I wish I had more answers for you."

He bowed his chin to rest on his steepled hands in sadness, while raising his eyes over the rim of his spectacles to watch the middle-aged man sitting across his desk in front of him, angry at the world.

"I don't know what business it is of yours," Nathaniel said curtly, standing. "I still don't know why my father left me here and didn't take me with him. I hated my mother. I hated everything about this town. My feelings haven't changed."

Silence followed Nathaniel's statement. The air was charged with hostility.

"I'm sorry to hear that," said Adam gently. "Just as I'm sorry you've blamed your mother for something she had no control over. She was expected to clean up after the fact and deal with any gossip, as if it was her fault. The woman is not always to blame, you know?" Adam stated as he stood.

"As you know, small towns have long memories about the bad things that happen. But no one ever knew the details about it. Your grandpa Gunther, Benjamin, and the sheriff made sure of it. Now that I've found out the sheriff's widow may have some knowledge, you may wish to talk with her."

Nathan shook his head no and pointed at his watch with resentment. "I need to go and don't have time for this wild goose chase. My mother was wrong and that's all there is to it!" His hostility hadn't abated.

"I would recommend that you talk with your father. I realize he's not a forthcoming man. But that would be the place to get your answers. You're lucky he's still alive and can answer your questions." Adam offered hesitantly. He stuck out his hand to shake goodbye.

Nathaniel quickly shook it and let out a long sigh. His tone now more agreeable, he said, "This whole thing is such a mess. It seemed like my mother was in the middle of all of it. The mess with grandma Catherina and the farm, the issue with my father, and ..." Nathaniel's voice trailed off.

He paused, looking at the man who had been his uncle Benjamin's best friend.

"Instead of traveling back to LA, I'll go to see my father in Boston," Nathaniel said suddenly. "It's been hard growing up with lies. He's a weak man and has lied for so many years. But I thought she was lying too and hated her for it."

Adam said kindly, "There's probably a good reason. Listen carefully."

"I will. It'll be the last time I'm able to see him since I heard he's dying of cancer as we speak," Nathaniel said as he opened the door to leave.

Nathaniel paused and turned to say, "But, first, I'm going to visit my grandma. She and my grandpa were my rocks when I was younger. Thank you. I'm sorry for my negative tone … I've lived with all these lies for too many years."

Before Adam could say anything, Nathaniel turned and purposefully walked out. Then he drove out to the old farmhouse to see his beloved grandma.

Catherina and Nathaniel –
May 17, 1950

When Nathaniel arrived at the old farmhouse where his mother had grown up in and his grandmother still lived, he was shocked at how old the place looked. It wasn't the neat showplace it had been years ago. But he hadn't been there in over a decade.

He inhaled the smells of freshly plowed fields and nodded at the man driving the tractor. The farmer was making his turn at the end of one row and moving on to the next row, turning up the soil. He looked up at the faded Gunther & Sons sign on the once red barn. The weathered boards were falling down, board by board. Only the two silos stood erect and seemingly unchanged. He remembered he was very young when the second silo had been built and had been a source of pride for his grandpa.

He recalled the time he spent helping his grandpa George, uncles, and cousins during harvest. He'd loved coming out to the farm as often as he could but knew being a farmer wasn't for him. The knowledge of farming helped him in his current job as an accountant working with farmers owning large produce farms in California and Arizona.

After knocking loudly on the side door leading into the kitchen, he opened it.

As he hesitated to allow his eyes to adjust to the lack of light, he saw his grandma Catherina and grinned. She was rocking in her old wooden rocker staring out to the backfields watching the dirt being rejuvenated for another year. It didn't appear that she'd heard his knock, so he said modulated his voice to say hello and not startle her.

"Oh, hello ..." Catherina said with a half-smile. Her whole face lit up when she recognized her visitor. But her eyes were sad. Even though Magdalena and she hadn't gotten along for most of their lives, she never thought of her children passing away from this life before her. It wasn't right.

"Come here ..." Catherina commanded as she struggled out of her chair. He waited patiently for her and then was rewarded with a big hug. She had shrunk and seemed small and frail.

He patted her back as he hugged her and allowed her to cry. He loved his grandmother. She'd always been kind to him and made him the best raisin cookies when he was a kid. He'd loved playing checkers with his grandpa. He remembered they'd enjoyed listening to him play the piano. Then he remembered receiving a note from her offering him the piano, which still sat dusty in the corner of the living room.

"What brings you out here?" Catherina asked, after returning to her rocker. "Come to fetch the piano?" She snickered.

He grinned and started to say, "I don't play anymore ..." when he saw a handsome black cat with golden eyes and white whiskers peering out from under the old checkerboard table.

He knelt and put his hand out for the cat to sniff. "Who's this?"

"That's Blackie. He's not sure if you're friend or foe," Catherina said. Then, added, "He viewed your mother as a foe."

Nathaniel had grinned and nodded. His mother forbade animals in her home, especially cats. She was never able to say why she hated felines so much. He stood and then pulled up a straight-backed chair from the old trestle kitchen table.

His grandmother said, "It was a nice service for your mother." Nathaniel agreed. They talked a bit about the funeral and the large number of people who had attended.

Finally, Nathaniel gathered up the courage to ask the questions he needed to have answered. He began hesitantly, not wanting to open any old wounds.

"I have some questions I hope you can answer … but I don't know how to ask them," Nathaniel started, haltingly.

Catherina waved her hand in the air. "You know you can ask me anything. I'll answer if I can." She turned sideways in her rocker so she could look directly at him.

"It's about my father … him leaving … so long ago." Nathaniel stammered, watching his grandma's face closely. He remembered his grandpa George forbidding any talk about that time.

"I don't know," Catherina said. She shrugged. "I don't know what happened. Your grandpa never said. I asked once and he shrugged and shook his head. I didn't ask again so as not to trigger one of his coughing spells."

"This is what Adam said …" Nathaniel shared all he knew.

"It's news to me …" Catherina said, her voice trailing off. "But it does make sense, given all the secrecy. Your father and his father left so fast. I believe it was in the middle of the night according to your mother. It devastated her.

"I know your grandpa Gunther helped her with the store for several years until she got both feet under her and even loaned her money. It was a big undertaking after the divorce. Living in town that was in a rural county wasn't easy as a divorced woman … and as a woman owning a store. She also raised you without help from your father. And, being blamed but not knowing what had happened. The rumors hurt. Now, you're telling me she wasn't even involved. I guess that explains why she was so angry so much of the time."

She then asked, "Have you talked with the sheriff's wife?"

Nathaniel shook his head. "I thought I'd fly to Boston and confront my father once and for all. It's time he told the truth. I don't need more hearsay."

"I hope he's able to tell the truth … it was so long ago," Catherina said. She'd never trusted Nathan to tell the truth and hoped he'd changed over the years. And memories changed over time too. She doubted he'd ever learn the whole truth.

They sat in companionable silence for a long time, feeling lighter. Then, Nathaniel stood and leaned down to hug his grandma goodbye.

"I'm sorry you and my mother didn't get along … but I love you. I forgive you for whatever you need to be forgiven for … hopefully you can do the same for me." Nathaniel kissed her wrinkled cheek and gently wiped away her tears and his.

"I love you, too," Catherina whispered in his ear. "God bless you. Let me know what you find out. I'd really like to know before I pass," Catherina said sadly. She feared it was the last time she'd see him.

"I will. I'll come back here one last time just to see you and let you know what my father says," Nathaniel promised. He watched her sitting so old and frail and so alone. He wanted to lighten her burden … one he still blamed his mother for causing … the loss of this grandparent's pride and legacy. His heart ached. This woman had lived an extraordinary life.

Before he turned to walk out, he saw a light from behind him. He turned to see his uncle Charlie standing in the open doorway. They gave each other a two-fingered salute.

Charlie whispered as he moved past his uncle to go outside, "You know, she insists on living here until the day she dies."

Nathaniel nodded.

As he sat in the car looking at the ruins of the old tenant home and at the run-down farm home where his grandma lived alone, he thought, *It's so sad to see everything looking so forlorn, even with the promise of a new planting and harvesting season as the tractors and plows turned the soil for another year.*

He shook his head as he put the car in gear. "You live and build a life … then, die," he whispered to himself. "I just want to be sure my life matters, and my family's legacy too." His hope was his father could remove those barriers by telling the truth.

Nathaniel and Nathan – May 20, 1950

After several days of travel and inquiries, Nathaniel found his father in a private Boston hospital.

He gave a half-smile at the old man as he lay there in the bed, thin and bald, a far cry from his memory of a lanky man with a full head of hair that he kept carefully combed and greased back.

At first, Nathan didn't recognize his son since he'd rarely seen him after leaving Harrison. When he did, he began coughing.

"To what do I owe this honor of my son visiting me?" Nathan spoke slowly and carefully so as not to trigger another coughing spell. "You look like my pa. I thought maybe I'd died, and he was waiting.

"But I'm not dead yet and it's been a long time," he added with a little humor, only to start coughing again.

After he stopped and took a sip of water, Nathaniel said, "I need to know about what happened *that* night." Nathaniel carefully replaced the cup of water on the table next to his father's bed.

"Why?" Nathan asked as he laid back in his bed. "It was so long ago." He didn't need to ask his son which night he was asking about. It had been like a festering wound that never healed. He'd hoped leaving a small town and moving to a large city would erase those memories. But they hadn't. Now, they were regrets that failed to go away.

"Yes. And. It's hurt my life."

"How?" Nathan asked, rasping. His bushy eyebrows were drawn together in surprise. "You've become a successful accountant. You make a lot of money. You told me several years ago that you're married with two sons and a daughter. That sounds like a great life."

"But you left me."

"Hmm ... I didn't leave you. I left an impossible situation." Nathan sighed and closed his eyes to rest.

Finally, with as much courage and strength, as he could muster, he opened his eyes. He looked into the eyes of his son for the last time. He finally told the truth ... or at least as much as he was willing to admit.

"I wasn't faithful to your mother. I blamed her for our getting married too soon. I thought I'd have the summer to play. But she insisted we get married on the same day that her parents had in July. My father agreed and performed the ceremony. I never understood the rush.

"I only married her because she was a hard worker and good with numbers. And because of the Gunther name. My father said she would be the best choice since we were still considered new in town and my father wanted to build a bigger congregation.

"While the Gunthers were not as wealthy as we, they were closer than many that lived in that town. My father hoped their good reputation would rub off on us." He paused to gather strength to continue in his confession.

"A year prior to the poker game I was at a hotel in Chicago. I enjoyed the company of a lady of the evening. Her name was Jillian. It lasted three days. I thought the affair was done and over when I left to return home."

He paused with tears in his eyes as he recounted that fateful night that changed the course of his life.

"The night of the poker game, a year later, Jillian showed up. Told me I had a daughter and wanted money to stay quiet. My father and I refused.

"So, she started yelling at us and threatening to tell everyone. You know small towns and gossip. I walked out the back of the parsonage and into the backyard to cool down. I needed time alone to think about what to do. But she followed me and grabbed my arm. I shook her off ... she fell ... hit her head on a large rock. I prayed she died instantly." He closed his eyes, remembering that evening.

"We all had had too much whiskey, including the sheriff. It appeared she had died since she wasn't moving or coming to," he said. "The sheriff told us that we needed to get out of town forever or he'd arrest me for her death.

"He covered her with a blanket and put Benjamin in jail as a witness so he wouldn't leave with us before riding out to get your grandpa Gunther. Adam had already left ... we could hear the train whistle its departure to Chicago.

"The two of them did whatever they did to erase the scene. I'd heard she'd been buried in a pauper's grave and have no reason to doubt what the sheriff told me. Benjamin was threatened and sworn to secrecy. But I left town and never returned. My father left with me since as a preacher he couldn't be caught in a scandal ... especially the death of a woman of dubious character."

He paused before adding, "We didn't know who Jillian really was or who her family was. We feared they might come looking for us since she had told me she had two older brothers and they worked for an important man in the city … whatever that meant. I don't know it for a fact."

"I thought Grandpa Landes was buried as a pauper," Nathaniel said, confused.

"No. He left me a lot of money. It's all gone … you know these medical expenses. The house is mortgaged to the hilt. No savings. But you already have money … so don't expect anything from me," Nathan said sadly. He closed his eyes again to rest.

Nathaniel asked in anger, "Do I have a half-sister? What's her name? Is she going to shake me down? What about your will? Who's the beneficiary?"

"I don't know. I've never heard anything from anyone," Nathan said. "I don't have Jillian's last name. My will is with my attorney."

He opened his eyes. His voice struggled, "I don't have any money. The little that is left will pay my medical bills. The bank owns the house. There's nothing left for you. I didn't include you in the will since you said you had your own money. Anything of value is gone. I just want to die a peaceful death."

Nathan then whispered, "I'm sorry. I know you came to see me. But I need to rest now. You know the truth. Go and live your life … leave me be. I can't help you live a happier life."

Nathaniel sat with his whole body shaking as he watched his father fall asleep. *All these lies. So many years of lies. For what purpose?*

He felt like crying but forbade himself from doing so. *She's still wrong and I refuse to forgive her. She could have found out the truth if she really wanted to know.*

He shared his father's confession with his grandma several days later before returning to his home and family in LA. They both felt relieved by the truth, even though there was nothing they could do to change the past and fix the tragic impact it had caused.

But as the two of them ate their last meal together, they questioned what had really happened to the woman who had caused the ruckus and changed so many lives. It was hard living in a small town to keep secrets and nothing had ever been said about that night, only gossip circulated about why Nathan and his father left in a big hurry. Both believed there was still more to the story that Nathan wasn't telling.

After Nathaniel left, Catherina rocked and prayed, "I hope he can forgive his mother someday and find peace, just like I've learned to do."

Rachel – June 1950

It was Rachel's second visit to Harrison after Maggie's funeral. This time she stayed with her ma and made the best of the porcelain potty situation. Maggie's home had been bequeathed to a charity and named Maggie's House under her recommendation and that of the women who were selected to be on the board with her, along with Adam as their banker and legal counsel.

After that visit, she decided it was easier for her to stay with Cora and Adam since they lived in town and had indoor plumbing. They were also close to Maggie's House and made it easier for her to take care of issues as they arose. Both were willing to lend her their car or drive her wherever she needed to go.

This gave her more time to spend with her ma. She'd even take Catherina with her to Maggie's House to see the progress of making over the house and answer any questions the board had about her oldest daughter.

It was during her second visit in June that Catherina asked her to get a box hidden in her bedroom under several layers of blankets in her cedar chest. The old, overstuffed cigar box and cover were worn, wrapped in bailing twine.

When she handed the box to Catherina, her ma held the box to her heart for several minutes. Then, said with tears glistening in her eyes, "You were closest to Benjamin." She handed her the box.

"Please keep these safe. I don't want someone else getting ahold of them. I fear what they would do to his memory.

"Benjamin was a great writer," Catherina said. "His death is my second greatest regret. I wish I could have traveled with him, but it would have been impossible since I was in my seventies. He wouldn't have wanted his old ma slowing him down." Catherina gave a half-smile.

Rachel nodded and stayed silent. She already knew her choice to leave Harrison had been her ma's third greatest regret.

Rachel carefully placed the box at the bottom of her luggage. When she was back in her new home in Albuquerque, she opened it and gasped at what she saw! The box contained all the letters Benjamin had written to their ma, plus an envelope containing several pictures.

Over the next several days, she savored the stories, happy chronicles of everything he'd seen and was experiencing. But they didn't reveal what had happened to him years ago.

She organized the letters by date and put them into a scrapbook. Then, she replaced the old, frayed envelope that held the pictures and selected the best one to paste on the cover of the scrapbook.

As she gazed at his picture, she thought about her own travels. *I wish I could have written like he could about my own travels.*

I'll give this album to Susan before I die since she loves traveling too. I hope she'll enjoy her uncle's stories.

After Maggie had passed, she still felt guilt about her family's name being tarnished and not having done something about it.

But, as Albert reminded me several times before his death in 1935, my family valued money and owning property above anything and anybody else … including our family. It was their way of feeling in control. It's why they weren't interested in the truth or the consequences of their greed.

But Rachel largely rose above her family's woes. When Albert was alive, they traveled to Chicago and New York City to see shows and museum openings. After he passed, she joined travel groups and took trips to Europe and Asia; Japan was her favorite spot. Sometimes Susan, Emma, and/or Grace would join her on one of her trips, all expenses paid. One summer between teaching assignments, Emma joined her for a trip to Sedona, Arizona.

There was no sadness about her choices. She felt blessed to be able to live her life the way she wanted. Her only regret was her family's unwillingness to be happy for her and supportive of the choices she made.

She was surprised to feel compassion for her ma. It was long overdue.

It happened after Maggie's funeral, when Rachel was packed and ready to leave.

Catherina said, "I love you. Be safe and take care if I don't see you again."

Surprised by her ma's outburst, Rachel turned around and went back to hug her ma goodbye for a long time.

Over the next few months, a stronger relationship grew between mother and daughter, although Rachel never confided in having been married or becoming wealthy. It was too personal and she didn't want to tear apart the fragile threads she was rebuilding by not having told her sooner.

With Rachel visiting more often, life changed for the better for Catherina. It was less lonely, and she grew more comfortable sharing her stories over the summer. These were stories that hadn't been told because George had been the storyteller.

After hearing one of them, Rachel encouraged her brothers and their families to come and visit and listen.

Catherina – Summer and Early Fall of 1950

"Tell me a story ..." her kids, grandkids, and great-grand-kids would say. They sat in a half-circle around her and the old wooden rocker. It made her giggle with glee that they wanted to hear *her* tell stories!

Catherina spoke of being a first-generation American and how her pa, their great-grandfather Papa Henry had left famine-stricken Germany for America with his younger brother, Josef (later changed to Joseph), and an older cousin. Papa Henry had been fifteen when Johann Wilhelm inherited the family farm as the eldest son.

Papa Henry and Joseph arrived in Philadelphia later that year and made their way westward over the next several years until they arrived in Berlin, Ohio. Their cousin had become ill and passed away on the ship.

Along the journey, they worked for meals and beds as farmhands. The few coins they earned, they saved for their future farms. It was a dream both had been telling each other every night as they waited to fall asleep. Eventually, they settled on adjoining farms in Berlin, a new German Methodist village in northwestern Ohio. There they met and married local German girls.

"They prospered and did well, until the year the cholera breakout took the lives of so many in their community," Catherina said. "It was when my mama and my two younger sisters died. I became the caretaker for my papa and uncle, and my two younger brothers, until they left home."

She smiled telling them about Papa Henry and the big red barn welcoming him when he first arrived to live in a small Pennsylvania town to harvest corn for a month. "I can't remember the name of the Pennsylvania town. He always said, 'I want one of those!'

"In my heart, our red barn signified our family's success … our ability to help fulfill my Papa Henry's dream and your grandpa George's dream too. That's why your grandpa and I made sure our big barn was red and the Gunther & Sons name was painted in large bold white letters so that everyone could see!"

The kids would ooh and aah before running to the window to look out at the once red barn, now falling down.

After they settled back down, she would continue.

"Your grandfather and I married on July 4, 1884, and celebrated with the Gunther family, my Papa Henry and uncle Joseph, and local farmers and church members. The next day, everyone was back to work."

She talked about George's family and her family speaking the language of the old country, with different dialects depending on where their ancestors had come from. "At first it was difficult for George and me to always understand each other when we spoke German, but over the years we'd learn to overcome these differences."

Then, she told the stories about traveling to Harrison, Illinois from Berlin, Ohio. "Your grandpa George bought this farm by Harrison in the fall of 1885. It was a very small village and the farm was only 200 acres at that time. George believed it was a great location because due west of here was the West Northern Railroad and Red Fox River. It made it easy to get our grains and corn sold.

"In March of 1886, we arrived after traveling by covered wagon. Your grandpa didn't trust travel on the trains. When we got here, we create a little field for garden vegetables along with planting big fields of corn and oats that first year.

"I never saw my beloved Papa Henry again. He had passed away later that year during a sudden and early blizzard in October. He had been bringing home the cattle that had wandered off his farm. I wasn't able to go back home for his funeral since we didn't hear about his passing until months later. Uncle Joseph died a couple of months after Papa Henry."

"I learned the details of Papa Henry's death by the only letter received from my youngest brother. It stated they buried Papa Henry in the German Methodist cemetery next to my mama and two sisters.

"The letter had requested money for a headstone for him. George had sent them money, but we never received a thank you. According to Benjamin when he visited years later, there was no headstone, and the rumor was they'd used the money to get out of town by jumping on a train and went east. According to the bank, my two younger brothers lost both farms and their store when the bank threatened foreclosure. No one knows where they went.

"In 1927 your grandpa George had several strokes. I cared for him with the help of family and neighbors. Your uncle Matthew moved here with his family to help us keep this farm. Then after your grandfather passed away, Matthew and his family moved to a small town southwest of Chicago."

When she paused, her hands, out of habit, patted the back of her head to make sure any stray pure white hair had not escaped its bun.

"When I was 16, I wanted to cut my hair short. But my mama admonished me for such fanciful thoughts. She told me that long hair was one of the greatest assets to attract a man."

When her burn mark peeked out from under the long sleeve of her dress on her left arm, she showed it to them. "This happened the day after my mama died and two days after my two younger sisters all died from cholera and were buried. I was cooking the noonday meal over the fire in the fireplace and because I was crying, I didn't notice the sleeve of my dress catching fire.

"Papa Henry doused the flames with a small basin of water used to wash hands and faces while yelling at my two younger brothers for adding too much wood. They were upset by Papa Henry yelling at them. It's probably why they left a year later since they never forgave their Papa Henry for making them work while grieving for their mama and little sisters. After they left, I never saw them again."

She told the story about the day Matthew's second-eldest daughter, Emma, beat her grandpa George at checkers.

"Your aunts and cousins said Emma should have let her grandfather win out of respect. After all, he was an invalid. But I suspect it was just jealousy since they couldn't beat him themselves."

While telling her stories, she'd mimic the people in the story. Her audience would clap and laugh.

With each retelling of her stories, she focused more and more on the good years. While those years were over too fast and gone forever, the happy memories brought a smile to her face and to her audiences and diminished the regrets and sadness they used to cause.

The kids would applaud and loved learning about their heritage. The sadness of any of these stories was replaced in time and became folklore for them to remember.

Their parents would roll their eyes when listening too, and snicker at her embellishment of the truth, especially about Matthew.

Rachel and Catherina – November 2, 1950

"Do you know my greatest regret in this life?" Catherina asked Rachel as she held up her hands to view the brown spots in the sunlight.

They were dressed up in their Sunday best and waiting for Cora and Adam to pick them up. Catherina hadn't been to Peoria in many years. The four of them were driving there for a late lunch and shopping. Her walking stick was by the door so she wouldn't forget to take it with her.

Rachel shook her head. "You have told me about your regrets with Papa Henry, Benjamin … and my choosing to not live in Harrison."

There was a moment of silence before Catherina continued, "My greatest regret began when George died in 1939 and his hoped-for legacy died with him. I wonder if he thought to himself, "Hey … wait a minute … I'm not ready. I have a promise to fulfill.""

They each sat with their thoughts, before Catherina said, "I knew George, Matthew, and I had an agreement … an irrevocable promise. It wasn't written down since the agreement was between family members. We shouldn't have needed one. Our word was our bond."

Rachel looked down at her hands before replying hesitantly, "I guessed that … that the promise was true."

Catherina looked over at her youngest daughter. She watched Rachel sitting as still as a statute before saying, "Why didn't you say something at the time?"

Rachel started to become defensive. Stopped. Breathed. Then, she said, "Maggie wrote me about it *after* you'd signed the will. I was told by Adam there was nothing I or anyone could do unless *you* made the changes."

Catherina murmured, "I wished I could have done more."

Rachel nodded and stayed silent. *What was done was done. There was nothing anyone could do to change it now.*

They silently watch the once colorful October leaves now turned brown dance in the November breeze.

After a few moments, Catherina whispered, "At first your pa used the excuse that it would hurt Peter's feelings and splinter the family further. That's why he wouldn't put the promise in writing. Then, after the sow incident, he feared people would stop visiting him."

She paused.

"Your pa loved all his children. But he loved the positive attention from his grandchildren and neighbors the most. Everyone thought of him as a kind old man. They would bring him stories, gossip, and food. Their visits gave him something to look forward to during all those years of lying in bed."

She paused again before adding, "I remember him saying to Matthew, 'You have to live in the same community with your brothers.' It was your pa's response to Matthew and me when we'd remind him to put his promise in writing."

Rachel asked, "Didn't pa remember the stories and … the feelings of betrayal when his own pa wouldn't give him the old Gunther farm back in Ohio?"

Catherina kept rocking and spoke softly, "I don't know. He stopped telling those stories after he was confined to bed. But several times at night when we were sitting in front of the fireplace, he would yell, out of nowhere, 'At least, I didn't follow tradition and give it to my oldest son. I'm giving it to the most deserving son.'"

"Why did he put the deed in your name?" Rachel asked a few minutes later.

Catherina shrugged, "I guess he hoped that would prevent him from having to do the right thing."

A minute passed before Catherina added, "Your pa believed the promise would be honored at the right time! He'd admonish me to 'Just leave it be.' He hated to be reminded of his promise, and the longer time went on, the more agitated he'd get when reminded."

Yet, the outcome had been the same, thought Rachel. *A family forever splintered by a legacy unfulfilled because pa hadn't had the courage to do what he had demanded of his own pa. Again.*

They heard Adam's car driving up the long drive to the old farmhouse. They quickly gathered their purses and coats. Rachel grabbed the walking stick Catherina had forgotten by the door.

Catherina – November 4, 1950

When she awoke from her short nap, Catherina smiled, remembering that Armistice Day and her oldest granddaughter Susan's birthday were coming up.

When Rachel arrived for their day together, Catherina told her about her joy in sending family members cards on their birthdays and on holidays. When her neighbors moved and others became too old to take her into town, she'd stopped. She missed the fun day of shopping and gossiping, getting out of the house when the old-timers were able to sit with George and chat and guffaw the afternoon away. She missed the pleasure of sending out the pretty cards.

"Did you know that even though Magdalena owned the store, she refused to bring me cards?" Catherina had asked Rachel during her last visit.

She'd mimicked Magdalena, "You need to send out cards to all your family, not just the thief and his children. Although why you'd send him and his kids anything is beyond me after what they did. It's a sin!"

"So, that's why you stopped sending cards!" Rachel said.

They both smiled remembering Magdalena's fearlessness in voicing her opinions.

Yes, Magdalena had been a strong woman, just like her ma. It was sad Maggie took her anger out on her ma. They could have become strong allies and kept the family together, Rachel thought.

The next day, after Rachel had completed the business for Maggie's House, she took Catherina to the local drug store.

Catherina grinned when she saw the long line of cards on display and spent over an hour looking at them all.

"I feel like a kid in a candy store!" She exclaimed.

Rachel lost count of how many her ma bought.

Catherina – November 6, 1950

Lightning flashed. Catherina could feel the electricity in the air as the fall storm raged through the area. She rocked back and forth in slow motion counting, 1001, 1002. She stopped as the thunder rolled again. Soon she saw another flash of light in the sky and started counting again, 1001, 1002, 1003 … and then another boom.

At least it's moving on, she thought to herself. She continued her back and forth rocking. After surviving eighty-four years of storms, she remained calm and sighed, *It's just another storm.*

She had heard several small branches fall on the roof of the old farmhouse and knew Charlie would check on them tomorrow.

Blackie stretched out longer on her lap, hanging his head over her knee. He emitted a loud purr that rattled through his whole body before falling back into a silent sleep.

Creak … creak … creak. She barely heard the runners of the rocker move back and forth on the old wooden floor that had become marred and scratched from the daily back and forth motion.

She inhaled the damp, cold air. Moisture had gathered on the inside of the windowpanes from the sudden change in temperature.

During the past few days, daylight had been disappearing earlier. At night, the temperatures dropped dramatically, announcing the end of the daily warmth from the beautiful Indian summer of reds, golds, and oranges. They'd been especially beautiful to see this year.

She rubbed her cold hands up and down the sleeves of her dress. Her fingers crippled with arthritis found a couple of small holes where she had previously mended the dress. While she had two nicer dresses, she only wore them on the outings Rachel had arranged for them this past summer. It felt so good to get out and see things again.

The material of this dress isn't as soft as when I made dresses for my two daughters and me. It had some type of flower printed on it, similar to the old grain sacks we used to make dresses years ago.

She sighed, remembering that the old dress she was wearing came from Magdalena's store years ago. It wasn't because she thought she needed a new one. But Magdalena had insisted she did, and also gave her a sales receipt showing how much she owed her. While Catherina had dug the coins out of a canning jar to pay her, she'd shaken her head. *I thought it was a gift.*

Ahh … memories of Magdalena and her strict ideas of how things should be. Catherina said to herself, *I sometimes miss my oldest daughter, although the family has gotten along better this past summer than in a long, long time.*

She shivered and tugged at the edges of the knitted navy-blue afghan around her shoulders, hoping for warmth. But the cold drafts circulated in the room, and she continued to shiver as she rested her bony elbow on the worn wooden armrest of her beloved old rocker. She still marveled that it was identical to her mama's, the one they'd left behind in Ohio.

Catherina – November 8, 1950

Rachel had been a godsend. She organized having her brothers and their sons bring down items and clean out the upstairs rooms and attic. There had been some surprises since a couple of the boxes contained very old items from the previous owner she'd never seen. Other items had been given to her for safekeeping by families moving west in search of gold. There hadn't been time to see what was up there during the past decades with so many other things to do.

She smiled, thinking back over the past several months. Rachel's visits, every couple of weeks, became a welcome reprieve from all the long, lonely days since Matthew left. When Rachel was done handling business for Maggie's House, she'd take her into town or just talk with her. Life was now joyful.

Jacob and Merry, Charlie and Melinda, and Rachel arranged outings for the six of them. At times, they included Adam and Cora. She'd eaten a hamburger at the 1930s Diner and enjoyed her first chocolate soda. She'd attended her first movie and saw an animated cartoon about a cat. Charlie's granddaughter had given her a professional manicure, although it hurt her fingers. The family had even held a surprise outdoor picnic, an eighty-fourth birthday party in her honor.

Even though Magdalena had scoffed at holding a Thanksgiving dinner here in her home, Rachel, Merry, and Melinda arranged one for Sunday, November 19th so that Catherina's sons could enjoy a meal together on the big day with their families. Rachel planned to stay, and they would join Adam,

Cora, and her children's families in town on Thanksgiving Day. Rachel and she talked about Catherina living with her during the winter months in Albuquerque.

During Rachel's review of the items kept upstairs, she'd found 30 old dresser and table scarves that were imprinted with a design that no one had embroidered. One Sunday afternoon, Melinda, Merry, Jessica, and their granddaughters came over. Instead of using colorful threads to embroidery, Rachel showed them how to use liquid embroidery. The results were beautiful. During the following afternoons and evenings, Catherina completed them by crocheting lace-like edging. Each person was given one and the rest were donated to Maggie's House as auction items to raise funds.

Rachel had found old boxes with the name Constance Gunther written on top. They contained porcelain china, silver, and fine table and napkin linens. They had been placed up in the attic on Benjamin's last visit before he left on his journey. When the boxes were opened, there was a moment of awed silence. Benjamin had wanted to ensure the beautiful items once owned by his beloved wife weren't sold by the nephews. Catherina had forgotten all about them.

When Rachel asked Catherina what she wanted to be done with the bounty, she'd shrugged. Then she said, "You and your siblings divide everything up." Rachel, Merry, Melinda, and their daughters and granddaughters organized the items. Jacob and Charlie and their sons and grandsons brought down the old furniture. There was no bickering and everything that was wanted was taken after Catherina had Rachel set aside certain items in a side room. Catherina had whispered to Rachel, "Be sure Matthew gets these, and set aside items for Peter too."

The rest of the many items not taken were sold and the money given to Maggie's House, including the piano.

The women's charity had hosted a benefit on a Saturday night in September when they erected the sign, "Maggie's House." She and her family had attended and applauded Rachel after she gave her welcoming speech.

When Rachel asked Peter if he wanted anything or to attend any of the family events, he declined. So did Matthew. But Rachel kept six finished dresser scarves, one for each of Matthew's daughters and the other two for Peter's two daughters-in-law.

Rachel told her, "I'm surprised by the amount of money Maggie bequeathed to Maggie's House!" They had both nodded and smiled.

The family relationships had become fun. They actually laughed and people came to visit her again. She could now appreciate why George welcomed visitors and looked forward to their visits. Rachel even had the old dangling strips of wallpaper repasted, and the downstairs furniture and glass items were cleaned and polished. Everything gleamed with cleanliness. Her home felt good again and her spirit was happy.

Catherina – November 10, 1950

As Catherina rested her chin in the palm of her hand, she tipped her head to the side so she could look out the big picture window towards the backyard and fields.

Nature mesmerized her. While her eyes were eighty-four years old, she'd watched the blur of the once gold, red, and orange leaves, now turned various shades of brown, as they rustled across the cold ground. They'd danced from one side of the backyard to the other, swirling around the old willow tree. Then the wind would change direction and they moved around the old maple and oak trees on the other side of the yard. She'd think, *I wish I could move like that again.* George and she had enjoyed dancing at community and church events over the years.

She thought back to when they'd planted the trees as saplings a couple of years after arriving there. The trees were planted in a row to one side of the house to serve as a wind-break against blowing snow. They made sure there was an unobstructed view of the red barn, backyard and fields beyond. A set of pine saplings had been planted to the south of the barn, but she couldn't see them.

George had lain in bed during his last years just staring out at the fields. "It's all in the land," he murmured over and over. What exactly he meant by that statement she never knew.

Today, the trees towered above the weathered clapboard farmhouse. In a far distance, she could still pick out the backyard and backfields whenever the rays of sunshine broke through the dark sky. She smiled noticing the once-red barn, now falling down board by board. When it had stood proudly, it had signified past prosperity and hard work. Decades ago, they had hosted a picnic for local farmers who came to help them paint it. It had been a testament to her family and hard work that so many people showed up.

The old grandfather clock chimed eleven.

The sunshine had given up and darkness took over again. She watched large raindrops pelt against the large picture glass window and roll down the pane. A couple of loose shingles on the old farmhouse roof rattled every time a big wind gust blew.

She considered lying down on the old Jenny Lind bed and covering up with the still handmade blue and rose-colored quilt her daughters had made decades ago when they both lived at home.

But the effort to get up was too difficult. Even with Magdalena gone, she still feared being caught asleep in bed during the day. Rachel had assured her over the past few months it would be good to rest her eyes during the day. But memories of her oldest daughter threatening to use it against her as a sign of weakness still haunted her.

Back and forth in slow motion she rocked using her feet on the short step stool to control the speed. *Creak … creak,* the old wooden floorboards groaned.

When Magdalena had been alive, there'd been too much controversy over who would get my things. She'd have dictated who got what based on how she felt about them at the time.

But now, thanks to Rachel, I got to say how everything was divided and who it was given to. It was such a relief to not worry about it.

I'm proud of my oldest daughter for being so generous and creating Maggie's House. Rachel is a great administrator. My only wish was that Magdalena's generosity could have been extended to her entire family when she'd been alive.

Catherina – November 11, 1950

With pride, Catherina smiled, thinking about the Gunther & Sons farm. It had expanded over the years from 200 acres to 500 acres and became one of the larger farms in the county. That was until others bought out small and mid-sized farms and became mega-farm owners during and after the Great Depression.

Her thoughts were interrupted by Blackie meowing. He'd wanted to make his way back down to the armrest of the rocker and demanded her attention so he could sit on her lap. She reached over and put her hands on each side of his black furry face to rub it.

"Such beautiful gold-colored eyes you have." She'd whispered. He put his paw on her hand and she'd stop. Then, he'd bat at her hand to resume petting him. If she waited too long, he'd make a gruff, long "mrrow." It was a daily game they loved to play.

He was a great comfort these days and had started staying in the house when she had visitors.

Catherina grinned. *If Papa Henry could see me now, talking to a cat, he would have roared at such foolishness.* When she was nine years old, she'd wanted to keep a cat in the home, but he'd forbidden it.

Papa Henry had said, "Animals, like people, have their roles on a farm. They're not pets. Their purpose, like people, is to take care of each other so everyone can survive."

But after Blackie arrived at her back door, Catherina and Blackie adopted one another. He wasn't demanding of her and kept up his duties of seeking out mice to earn his keep during the nighttime hours. He kept her company during the long, lonely days before Magdalena passed. She still kept a glass bottle of milk in the icebox for him.

She snickered thinking about George's decree. *He'd sounded just like my Papa Henry.*

As Blackie watched her, she mimicked George, "There are enough mouths to feed and work to do. I will not worry about any animals in the house." This was after Magdalena and Rachel had begged to have the old brown tiger tomcat sleep with them.

"He can go eat mice and other rodents in the barn, and find straw or hay to keep warm. That's his job."

But the sisters had sneaked the cat into their bedroom. This continued until a few days later they were itching from flea bites.

After stopping her game with Blackie, she looked out the living room window.

Another November storm was brewing. There seemed to be a lot of them this year. She could feel it in her bones and could smell the rain coming. She could hear the wind rattling the loose shingles on the old farmhouse.

I've survived many a storm, she thought to herself. *God willing, I'll survive this one too.*

As the old rocker rocked back and forth creaking, she gazed down at the brown spots that covered her hands.

She whispered, "These brown spots are the regrets God bestowed upon me. Life's gone by too fast. It is too late to change anything. But I'm so thankful that I am now able to remember the good times too."

Catherina looked out the window to where she knew the fields were.

In her heart, she could see George gazing down upon his fields with a smile of satisfaction.

He'd see the brown cornstalks waving in the wind.

Or the drab yellow kernels of corn lying in a mound in the tracks left by the wagons during harvest.

Or the fields sparkling after the cold snow shower had moved through.

Or the November sun bidding goodbye to another harvest.

He'd then say, "We've sacrificed and endured all the hardships God meted out. It's now time for our heavenly reward."

She bowed her head in prayer and asked for forgiveness. *Please forgive me for not having the backbone to fight and fulfill George's promise. I was too old and too exhausted from taking care of him for so long. Please forgive George for denying his family the greatest legacy he could by honoring his promise to Matthew.*

As she closed her eyes, she shook her head to remove the memories of regrets and replace them with the recent good times. Faintly, she could feel Blackie's purrs vibrating against her thigh. She reached her hand down to stroke his velvet ears with the tips of her fingers. His feline grace purred his loudest providing her momentary relief.

Blackie nudged her hands with his cold, wet nose before moving onto her lap to stretch out. She gently ran her forefinger down his leg to his paw. Blackie turned his paw to capture her finger, careful to keep his claws from scratching her.

They held hands as she gradually relaxed and fell asleep.

When she awoke, she smiled remembering her dream of happier times when she was a little girl. The wildflowers she'd pick for her mama. Her little field and having her own money. The tears of her Papa Henry saying goodbye and giving her the gold coins.

As a sudden wind gust rattled the entire farmhouse, her heart stopped beating and her body relaxed. She heard the grandfather clock chime for the last time.

The soft white light of love radiated from her beloved Papa Henry and enveloped her. It was a welcome relief after so many years of regrets.

She exclaimed, "Papa! You've finally come."

Blackie sat up and calmly watched as the bright light left and ascended into heaven.

November 19, 1950

Rachel, Jacob, Merry, Charlie, and Melinda all raised their glasses of water in a toast to George and Catherina. They honored their parents' rule of no alcohol in the house.

As they shared the Thanksgiving dinner that had been originally planned for Catherina to enjoy with her children, they retold the stories about their ma and pa that they'd been hearing lately. Many were new to them.

"I'm sorry we didn't know about Ma's life before," Jacob said with tears in his eyes.

They'd done their best to heal the family strife that had simmered for so many years between them. During this past summer, even their ma had laughed and enjoyed herself instead of brooding about past regrets. They'd honored her wishes and gave away her furniture and other items. Jacob would sell the old family home that was part of his parcel when he was ready.

Matthew and Peter and their families had declined to travel to Harrison to join them for this Thanksgiving dinner. The olive branch had been extended, at least in the minds of Jacob and Charlie and their wives. But Rachel knew Peter and Matthew didn't view these efforts as olive branches.

Merry remarked, "Isn't it a coincidence the old red barn fully collapsing the day before we buried Ma?"

Before anyone could respond, Melinda asked about Blackie, "I've not seen him around since Catherina's funeral. Have any of you?"

Charlie looked down at his hands and said quietly, "I found him curled up in the old shed. He was dead. I buried him in ma's garden."

They raised their water glasses in tribute to their ma and Blackie, and to the red Gunther & Sons barn and all it had signified.

After the meal, Adam arrived in his new red 1950 Chevrolet pickup to get Rachel. The men loaded the old wooden rocker, footstool, checkerboard table, Jenny Lind bed, marble railroad, and several boxes containing other family items like the family Bible and their father's watch that Catherina had asked Rachel to keep in a small room in the back of the old family home.

When Adam drove out of the driveway, he turned left instead of turning right to go into Harrison.

Jacob exclaimed as he watched the dust stirred up from the road by the pickup, "Whoa! Where are they going? I thought they were taking those items to Maggie's House."

Melinda and Merry nervously giggled. "No. They are taking them to Matthew's house. Peter already claimed the items Catherina wanted him to have."

Jacob quickly adjusted his cap to hide the tears that had sprung in his eyes. The other three looked down at the ground, pretending to ignore Jacob's sadness over Matthew and the past.

In their mind, the family legacy was over with the death of Catherina. But in the hearts and souls of future generations, the family legacy was far from over and already being replayed.

Epilogue:
Nathaniel – November 19, 1950

Nathaniel had worked hard to control the interactions between him and his parents by ignoring and distrusting the two people that had brought him into this life. He was angry at both for the lies and troubles they caused for so many. His intention was to prevent them from causing any trouble for his family.

When he moved his family from Chicago to Los Angeles for work, his children had insisted on meeting his mother, their grandma Maggie. After a lot of badgering, he finally agreed. He also introduced them to his grandma Catherina. The visit went okay but was a tense two days. He was so happy to see the town of Harrison in the rear-view mirror.

He surprised himself by going back for the funerals, but it felt good to be part of the Gunther family again.

Nathaniel sat in his red recliner by the big window in his living room and flipped the footrest up to lie back in his chair. He reflected on Catherina's funeral and thought his aunt Rachel had done a good job with Maggie's House. He offered to provide financial and accounting services through his company in Chicago. The siblings seemed to get along better without his mother stirring up old feelings of discord.

He'd said all the right things while he was there but left exhausted by having pretended to be happy to see everyone and listen to their stories … many he had already heard too many times … yet some were new and good to hear.

When he'd returned home late on Saturday night, he'd told his wife, Linda, about everything that had occurred. This morning Linda and their three children had put together a big welcome home breakfast of Eggs Benedict with fresh fruit for him before leaving to attend church.

He declined to go with them to Sunday School at 9 a.m. and the church service at 11 a.m. Instead, he promised to join them for dinner at their favorite restaurant after they were done with church and their weekly visit with Linda's parents.

He sat up and turned his attention to the week-old Sunday edition of the *Boston Globe*. After reading the headlines, he flipped to the obituary page and was surprised to see his father's name listed. *I thought he'd already passed.*

As he read the obituary, his face turned from surprise to sadness to shock to anger.

It stated … *survived by wife Jillian and daughter Shasta.* His name was not mentioned.

He yelled, "What did he do now? More lies!"

Nathaniel hired the accounting and legal people from his company in Boston to uncover information about his dad and grandpa Landes, and to find Shasta and Jillian. It had taken a year and a half.

Shasta was living in Omaha and owned a car dealership along with someone named Dale Linkman. The information said he was her dad. Also, that Jillian Landes was deceased, and her maiden name was not included in the obituary.

Nathan went to see Shasta without letting her know beforehand.

But when he arrived and Shasta's secretary announced him, it was as though she had been expecting him. After shaking his hand, she put her finger to her lips, indicating not to say a word. After she invited him into her office, she had her secretary cancel all her appointments and popped open her safe to pull out a thin manila envelope.

With a nod towards the door, she said matter-of-factly, "Let's go."

To her secretary, she said, "Tell Dale to meet Nathaniel and me at the country club."

"We need to wait for Dale so he can fill in any blanks I cannot explain," Shasta said after they were seated far away from the other club members.

They ordered coffee, muffins, and fruit while making small talk. During this time, he learned she used his company in Chicago for their accounting work.

When Dale arrived and had his coffee served, she began the story.

"My mother's name was Jillian. She was Dale's wife. Dale had been a traveling salesman and moved us around the Midwest for many years. We lived in Harrison for six months during 1913. Before I turned one, we moved to Chicago and stayed. Dale found work selling cars at a dealership and was good at it. The owner liked him and offered to help him any way he could."

Dale sat listening and nodding as Shasta continued her story.

"For some reason Dale questioned my paternity."

He interrupted by saying, "I caught Jillian having an affair and she admitted she'd had several over the years when I was away from home working for weeks at a time."

Shasta picked the story back up, "My mother finally admitted my biological dad was Nathan Landes, a young man she'd had a fling with until his wife found out. Given that his wife was the daughter of a wealthy man in Harrison, they decided to keep the pregnancy secret."

She paused before adding, "I believe that was your mother."

Nathaniel shrugged and nodded. *He didn't know if it was true or if his mother knew.*

"When Dale kicked her out, Jillian wanted to rekindle her relationship with Nathan. So, she showed up in 1916 and found your father playing poker with his dad and several other men in the parsonage. When she threatened to tell everyone the truth, your father either backhanded her or she fell, depending on when she was telling the story and how much she'd had to drink. Your dad and grandfather Landes, fearful of any scandal and the consequences from Nathan's wife's family, scurried back to Boston."

Dale interjected with downheartedness, "I followed her from Chicago to Harrison to see who she was meeting since she was still my wife, and wanting to confront Nathan. But I never got the chance. I saw her fall and watched them cover her with a blanket and leave. It happened all so quickly. I picked her up and drove her back to Chicago. She had a slight concussion but was okay. I didn't see Nathan physically hurt her, but I couldn't see everything happening in the dark. There was only the light from the kerosene lantern shining from the back doorway."

Shasta continued unemotionally, as if she was addressing a board of directors, "A few months later, my parents divorced. Two months later, my mother dragged me to Boston and insisted Nathan marry her. He did. But he refused to acknowledge me as his daughter, pointing to all the other men she'd dated and claiming I didn't look like him.

"When I was old enough, and after writing weekly letters to Dale, I travelled back to Chicago after convincing my mother and Dale that I wanted to visit him. He had agreed to a short visit. I talked him into letting me stay and giving me a real home." She took a sip of coffee.

Then she added, "We're still not sure to this day if I'm really Nathan's daughter or Dale's or someone else's. But to me, Dale is my real dad and always has been.

"When your father died, my mother wanted to remind everyone that she was the wife, and I was the daughter by posting the obituary. I think she still believed there was a lot of hidden money to inherit even though your father told her there wasn't any. So, when she died two months later, I inherited everything there was to inherit. A house owned by the bank. Medical bills that needed to be paid by the sale of his classic cars, etc. I took what I wanted as keepsakes for my future kids before the bank took over and left everything else."

Nathaniel listened without comment. Then, he asked, "How bad were the medical bills?"

Shasta snickered, "Didn't you notice when you visited that he was in an expensive private hospital and a private room?"

Nathaniel shook his head. "I was too focused on getting answers."

Dale added, "He was born with a silver spoon in his mouth, and he wanted to die with one too."

Silence hung in the air and was only interrupted by the sounds of coffee cups and saucers and the clanging of silverware being used by other club members. Nathaniel sorted through the new information in his head and added it to what he'd already discovered. Everything was mostly as he had learned. Yet, something wasn't ringing true.

"I still don't understand why the need for secrecy. Since you knew who I was, why didn't you reach out to me?"

"I'm the one that inherited everything from my mother and there was nothing of any value to share. You were not listed in your father's will," Shasta declared.

Then she added after glancing at Dale, "The other reason was my dad and I traveled after I returned home to Chicago. One time we traveled through Omaha, and he noted that it would be a great place for a dealership."

Dale picked up the story, "So I told her to get her college degree. She would run the place and I would handle the day-to-day sales and service. But to get the Cadillac dealership in a small, growing city they wanted someone with moral fortitude. So, it's important that we were father and daughter … they checked those types of things. Also, the owner of the dealership in Chicago put in a good word for us since Shasta worked part-time for the dealership when attending college."

Shasta added, "We didn't know what you'd do or say."

They were all quiet for a few minutes.

"Didn't the obituary hurt that image?" Nathaniel asked. He found that their story was too well-rehearsed. Also, he suspected there was a leak in the Boston office since most of what they were sharing he already knew.

"No. We explained Nathan was my step-dad and my mother was overcome by grief." Shasta said. "Plus, my birth certificate had Dale's name listed."

"They accepted it," Dale added.

Shasta pushed a manila envelope towards him. "Here are the documents that you may wish to review. They show the foreclosure of the property and the bank accounts being empty. There is no money left in the estate; it was closed after my mother died. There is a smaller envelope in there with $500 in cash that I found in his safe. There were no letters or anything of a personal nature."

Nathaniel pushed the big envelope back at her; he had already had copies mailed to him by his Boston office since they were public documents. "I don't need the money or want to know what else is in the envelope," he said. "Please give the money to a local charity. It's not why I pursued this. I wanted … needed … the truth … or as much as humanly possible. I'm tired of the lies I endured during my lifetime about what happened when my father abandoned me."

Dale said carefully, "Sounds like it was a good thing, given his inability to care for anyone other than himself. Looks like your mother and family did a good job. Look at all you've accomplished."

Nathaniel gazed at him. *He had a point.*

Shasta pushed the envelope back at him. "I would recommend that you read the papers for posterity's sake. Burn them. I don't care. I've moved on and I recommend you do too."

"Do you know who your biological father is?" Nathaniel asked. *She doesn't look like either my dad or Dale with her red curly hair and petite stature.*

Shasta shook her head. "But it doesn't matter. Dale is my dad. I know it could have been several other men she had flings with. But I'll never know. I've forgiven my mother. I'm getting married next month and will become a step-mom. I don't want my past getting in the way of helping those kids through the trauma of a bad divorce. Those kids will have enough to deal with having a new parent and listening to their mom trash me even though she was the one that strayed from the marriage."

She paused before adding with a half-smile, "And, you and I think we had it bad!"

They sat for a moment while she reached over and squeezed Dale's hand with affection.

Nathaniel nodded and stood. He was done and knew he'd hit a wall. Whatever his father had been involved in was not going to be told to him. Time to let it go. He shook hands with each of them and purposely left the envelope on the table.

They are hiding something ... but I'm never going to learn the whole truth. Or it could be they didn't really know. Memories are never the whole truth.

As he sat in the terminal at the airport waiting to board his flight, it hit him.

I need to forgive my mother. I'm sorry for how I treated her … she deserved much better from me after all her sacrifices and struggles.

My hope is that my daughter, Sybella, can become a strong woman like my mother. I need to stop being so harsh and critical about her speaking up.

After Nathaniel left, Dale asked softly, "Do you think he bought it?"

Shasta shrugged while shaking her head. "It doesn't matter. He's not going to pursue this any further. Family matters can be the end of us if we let them fester. He's not going to do that, or he would have taken the envelope."

About the author

About the book

P.S.

About the Author

Jeannette Seibly reconnected to both the paternal and maternal sides of her family in 2000. She found it fascinating to discover how the ancestral stories were interwoven generation after generation! Because of this work, and her experience and education, she's shared with friends and clients these stories over the years. Doing so helped many of them make different choices that improved the quality of their family interactions.

Hailing from a pioneering family in Michigan, Jeannette loves living in sunny Colorado with her cat, Gracee in the shadow of the scenic Rocky Mountains.

This book is not an autobiography. It has taken over 20 years to develop and write after working through my family's inherited biases and judgments and releasing my own. But these elements are not limited to my family. All families experience these legacies.

When I was in 9th grade, I wrote a story about an old woman sitting in an old wooden rocker. In the story my character gazed out a window, recounting her regrets. Now, after exploring a lot of my family's history, that makes sense. I found the stories fascinating (e.g., why two brothers excluded each other in their obituaries, why a man would drive by and wave at his wife every Sunday as she walked to church that was along his way, uncovering a story written a century ago about my family history that was not true, etc.). We can never know the truth of what was in the hearts and minds of our ancestors at the time.

These are our legacies. It takes strength and courage to create new and empowering ways of interacting with each other in our families. It is my wish that we understand our family history and learn how to love and accept one another as we are, not as we believe we should be.

This book was possible due to the help and insights of many people, including Faye Kunkle Seibly, Diane Putvin, Karen Lillie, Mythica von Griffyn, Sue Simmons, Marisha Wozniak, and others who listened and shared their own stories. They were supportive during this long process of healing, discovering, and writing during the past two decades.

What are Generational Legacies or Prophecies?

We're all aware of how our DNA is a replication of our parents, their parents, and back through time. But not as well-known is how we inherit our communication styles; religious, monetary, and political beliefs; and societal mores, even when there is a deliberate intent to change them!

Many of us aspire to live a better life than our parents and grandparents. But the challenge is that ancestral conditioning shades our attitudes, actions, words, and inactions towards one another, especially family members. It's replayed throughout history and handed down in stories. Until we discover the truth, we cannot stop it.

Uncovering the truth allows us to make conscious choices. It sets aside the lies and innuendos many families create about one another. It heals familial wounds and provides acceptance. This is how family members stop breaking a family into pieces that cannot be mended.

True forgiveness requires awareness. It goes beyond ancestral trees, family newsletters, periodic reunions, and other connectivity attempts. These activities are a great start to bring family members back together and can start a familial healing process. But they are rarely enough.

First, we must discover the facts in our historical folklores and how they are being replayed today. We must accept that we will never know the whole truth of what happened, or why situations occurred, especially when we attempt to apply today's standards to past events.

Second, it's important to stop demanding that others adhere to a moral code set by one family member or group of family members. "If you don't do and say and believe what we tell you, you will not be accepted in this family!" needs to be extinguished.

Third, we must learn acceptance and forgiveness. It's how broken familial threads are repaired, and the tapestry can be made whole again.

How To Get Started

Trace your family threads and find your genealogical legacies

Tracing family history can be a fascinating and rich process of collecting research and coming to terms with one's family history or ancestry. To do so, one needs to pay attention to collecting and verifying facts, stories, and other information. Otherwise, it's too easy to latch on to someone else's story.

Fact gathering:

Classes—there are many workshops and seminars that can help clarify facts and differentiate facts from myths. These can save time, money, and wasted efforts to authenticate the family lineage.

Digitize—use a computerized system to collect data and pictures. This makes it easier to share results and find new connections. Don't forget to back up the information in the event of a computer crash or an upgrade to a new system. Keep information updated and be respectful of not sharing personal data of those still alive, regardless of where you found the material.

Genealogy records—verify the information found on the internet, history sites, family trees (online and private), religious records, genealogical websites, books, and family stories. There is a lot of misinformation written and posted everywhere.

Stories—find a way to authenticate the information whenever possible, particularly from generations ago. As historians will attest, stories may be simply stories and not the truth for the direct lineage of a family.

History—become aware of the era and the issues of that time period by reading history books and historical fiction, and watching movies and documentaries depicting the era. Become aware of the choices available due to societal mores and familial traditions of the time.

Newsprint and obituaries—can provide additional information. Again, find ways to authenticate the information whenever possible. Old newspapers frequently misspelled names, misstated facts, and omitted details.

Online chat groups—newly found distant cousins can provide information not readily available; don't forget to share responsibly.

Interviews, video and/or audio recordings—talk with parents, grandparents, aunts, uncles, former neighbors, etc. *now* before they and the information they possess is gone. Once it is gone, it's forever.

Access past family member's Akashic records—talk with someone skilled in accessing "The Akashic Records." This process can reveal things that otherwise are lost to history. Beware that someone's impression or view doesn't necessarily make it the truth.

Reading Group Guide

1. Traditions die hard, if ever. They create an illusion of family and determine how we act towards one another, or risk being removed from the family tree as the black sheep. Why was Rachel considered a "black sheep"? How come Peter and Benjamin were not also considered "black sheep"?

2. Have you been considered a "black sheep" in your family? Or, do you have a family member who is considered a "black sheep"? What happened to cause the situation? Why did it seem important at the time? What can be done to change the outcome today?

3. We're all aware that our DNA is inherited from our parents, their parents, and back through time. But many of us are unaware that our communication styles; religious, monetary, and political views; and societal mores are also a fated legacy of the past that continues unconsciously into the future. It's a family tapestry that thread by thread unravels over time. Can you see those threads in your family's tapestry? What is the primary thread holding the family together (e.g., religion, money, property, education, etc.)?

4. Do you believe Maggie's anger justified what she did to Matthew? Was it in the best interests of everyone? Or, was it an emotional reaction to being in control and having things done her way?

5. Was Matthew being selfish to expect to receive all 500 acres of the Gunther & Sons farm? Why?

6. What would you have done if George was your father and failed to put a promise made to you in writing?

7. Has your parent, or you, ever been in Catherina's position of being a caregiver? Following the death of a family member, were you the one expected to bequeath family items in a particular way? What worked about these expectations? What didn't work?

8. Everyone has dreams about what they'd like to achieve in their life. What dreams did you have when you were younger? Have you allowed family expectations to get in the way of achieving them? What can you start doing today to make your dreams a reality?

Further Reading – Excerpt from
A Mother's Greatest Regret

September 1948

As Patti traveled by train to Madison to attend college and live with her Aunt Rachel, she thought confidently about the major she'd already unofficially declared at the University of Wisconsin. It was to get her "Mrs." degree. The memories of wealthy ladies from Chicago traveling through her hometown of Haverhill, Illinois made her envious but determined to be like them. The first step was finding the right man.

She was excited about taking her turn living with her aunt, but was already at odds with Paulina, her favorite sister. It had been a long time since all four sisters had been together and she expected all of them to be there to greet her at the train.

But Susan had not been there … just Emma and Paulina. To cover up her disappointment, she made a comment about Susan's laziness. Emma overheard and was silent throughout the cab ride to Aunt Rachel's apartment. Paulina refused to look at her. *I'd better keep my thoughts about my two oldest sisters being spinsters to myself,* thought Patti. *But it's embarrassing; they're almost 30!*

When they arrived, Patti admired the beautifully set table with its white damask table covering, gleaming china, silver, and crystal. Two candle sticks stood tall in lead crystal vases. She hugged herself. This was luxury. She even had her own bathroom with running water. Yes, finding a rich man was definitely her goal.

While they ate, they discussed safe topics such as Madison politics and the classes Patti had registered for. Someone asked Paulina about Ralph's new job at the local bank and their wedding plans. Then the talk turned to Emma's plans, since she'd moved back to Madison for a teaching position.

Emma said with a smile, "I hope Mom and Dad are happy without children at home after so many years."

This triggered Patti. "Dad liked you best!"

Emma frowned and shook her head in shock. "What brought this up?"

Patti replied, "I tried to do things with him. He was never interested."

Susan and Paulina sighed loudly as a warning. Patti ignored them. Aunt Rachel quietly got up and left the table. The girls were silent until they heard her bedroom door shut quietly.

Paulina said nervously, "Dad loves all of us. You need to remember to watch what you say. We don't have room for you if you upset Aunt Rachel."

But Patti plunged on, oblivious to her poor manners.

"Yeah, but Emma was his favorite. The son he never had. All he ever talked about was how well she did in college. He really was proud of that women's softball team she made champions out of." Patti had felt ignored by her dad, even as the only child living at home. It hurt.

Emma quietly responded, "You played basketball, and he came to your games."

"His primary interest was listening to baseball games on the radio."

Emma caught herself before saying, *they don't play baseball and basketball during the same time of the year.*

"Yeah, but I didn't get all A's like you did!" she continued.

"All you had to do was study," Emma said.

"You never had to!" Patti replied.

"I didn't have to study to get good grades. I was lucky." Emma responded. "But I had to learn how to in college; it wasn't as easy as high school." *This is ridiculous! Patti had it so much better than the rest of us.*

Emma attempted to quell the situation. "I thought you went hunting and fishing with dad."

"Once! I could never bait a hook to his satisfaction. I hated touching slimy worms. While I can fire a rifle and hit the bullseye, I cannot hit a running deer. So, dad stopped taking me. I did win the girl's 4-H rifle competition at the fair this past summer. He did say he was proud but mentioned that you were an ace shot too."

Emma turned to see Paulina looking down at her plate, red-faced. She knew about Paulina and Patti kibbitzing about Susan and her … but this was too much.

Defiantly Patti said, "None of you were there to take care of them! It was all left up to me." She wanted to be treated as a grownup, not their little sister.

Paulina smiled graciously at her aunt, who was now standing in the doorway listening. She said, "Well, you really should consider yourself lucky. When we first arrived, Aunt Rachel was a saint, teaching us how to use all these modern-day things."

Rachel frowned as she listened. She'd hoped the time spent living in Madison would bring the four sisters closer together. They were eating dessert when Patti asked, "Guess who gave me money for graduation?"

They looked at her, surprised.

"Aunt Maggie!" Patti crowed with a big smile. The others sat, silent.

"Well, I don't care what anybody says. It wasn't any fun being the only one living with them. I worked just as hard as any of you. You weren't there to take care of them! I was."

Susan said quietly, "You really have no idea of how hard each of us worked to be able to survive the Depression and keep our grandparents' farm. You should be more respectful of your elders."

Patti glared at her. "How would you know? Everyone had to do your chores! It would be a good idea for you to get married! If anyone would have you!"

Everyone gasped.

Patti said defiantly, "I'm going to look for a rich man to marry."

Aunt Rachel quietly replied, "It's just as easy to marry a rich one as a poor one!"

Later in their apartment, Emma said to Susan, "Patti promised Mom she would behave."

"She's forgotten already!" Susan remarked. "It's only been eight hours! I hope Aunt Rachel has a lot of patience."

Susan asked, "Why do Patti and Paulina have such negative attitudes toward us?"

Emma shrugged, "I don't know. Maybe it's because we're single. They seem to think they're better than us."

Susan retorted, "Well, maybe they are. But I thought family was supposed to support each other. They're worse than our cousins were, growing up."

Emma shook her head and shrugged, "I know. I hope Patti outgrows it."

"Don't hold your breath," Susan responded.

The reunion had not gone well. The legacy of the sibling rivalries and jealousies of the past was beginning to encroach upon a whole new generation.

www.ingramcontent.com/pod-product-compliance
Lightning Source LLC
Chambersburg PA
CBHW021614270326
41931CB00008B/690